Crime and Women

About the Editor

Dr. R. G. Dastidar is a post-graduate from the Department of Sociology and Social Work, Bhopal University. A UGC JRF started a passion for research and writing which has become an on-going engagement with women and women issues as they are reflected in academics. She has worked on many projects researching various aspects of women, work and empowerment. In the course of her work in the Department of Sociology she also is a guide to various researchers. She is actively working with various NGOs as advisor and consultant. Underlining these activities is an attempt to document women's situations in its multiple social settings and to increase social understanding of the same. She has also published various research articles in academic journals and is an active participant in various conferences.

Her other academic interests include sociological theories and research methods.

Crime and Women

Edited by
Ruchi Ghosh Dastidar

CONCEPT PUBLISHING COMPANY PVT. LTD.
NEW DELHI-110059

ISBN-13 : 978-81-8069-810-1

First Published 2012

Published and Printed by

Concept Publishing Company Pvt. Ltd.
A/15-16, Commercial Block, Mohan Garden
New Delhi-110059 (India)
T: 25351460, 25351794, *F*: 091-11-25357109
E: publishing@conceptpub.com, W: www.conceptpub.com
Editorial Office: H-13, Bali Nagar, New Delhi-110 015, India.

Cataloging in Publication Data--*Courtesy:* D.K. Agencies (P) Ltd. <docinfo@dkagencies.com>

Crime and women / edited by Ruchi Ghosh Dastidar.
p. cm.
Includes bibliographical references and index.
ISBN 9788180698101

1. Women—Crimes against—India. 2. Family violence—India. 3. Women—Legal status, laws, etc.—India. 4. Women—India—Social conditions. I. Dastidar, Ruchi Ghosh, 1967-

DDC 362.880820954 23

प्रो. निशा दुबे
कुलपति
बरकतउल्ला विश्वविद्यालय
होशंगाबाद रोड, भोपाल-462 026
फोन : +91-755-2491701
फैक्स : +91-755-2491703
ई-मेल : nishadube.law@gmail.com
वेबसाइट : www.bubhopal.nic.in

Professor Nisha Dube
Vice Chancellor
BARKATULLAH UNIVERSITY
Hoshangabad Road, Bhopal-462 026.
Ph. : +91-755-2491701
Fax : +91-755-2491703
E-mail : nishadube.law@gmail.com
Web : www.bubhopal.nic.in

Foreword

Mahatma Gandhi once said, "All crimes are a kind of disease and should be treated as such". Hate crime and not the criminal. However, crime continues to be a challenge to our administrators and its distribution and pattern point to social malaises which may be traced back to their historical roots. Crime against women has special relevance as it challenges not only our future as a nation but also all the developmental gains we have made so far, not to mention the emotional appeal it has to a culture that has placed women very highly.

Gandhiji traced the problem to the seven blunders that human society commits and cause all the violence : These are wealth without work, pleasure without conscience, knowledge without character, commerce without morality, science without humanity, worship without sacrifice, and politics without principles.

It is a matter of grave concern that India is showing a high incidence of crime against women. According to 2009 NCRB report, 2,03,804 cases were reported of crime against women including both IPC and SSI's with a 4.1 per cent increase over previous year. The report also shows around 15,140 women in jail under all categories of convicts, under trials, detentions and others. Ongoing research in the area is needed and happily the present book is the outcome of one such effort.

Universities are in fact lively because of the flow of ideas and research is its backbone. I wish all the authors the very best and hope they will move on to take higher challenges in research and that their works will contribute to better understanding of society and the growth of knowledge. I am sure more such work on women and crime shall be coming from these authors.

Prof. Nisha Dube

Acknowledgements

This work would have been impossible without the help and support of my friends and well-wishers. I would like to acknowledge their help and convey my gratitude to them for their faith and patience. This project has taken a long time to be completed and more than its fair share of hiccups. I am happy to see it finally go to the publisher, hope it will be useful to future researches in this field, and give them valuable insights on crime and how it affects women. For some of us, this has been an opportunity to get to know each other better and share our academic concerns, most of all it has been a learning experience as we stepped beyond our class-room and offices, it has helped us all grow.

Thanks are due to our Hon'ble Vice Chancellor Dr. Nisha Dube,Barkatullah University for constant encouragement. To all my seniors and colleagues here in the Department of Sociology and Social Work, I acknowledge with gratitude the influence and support of Prof. Gautam Gyanendra, whose on going and valuable discussions continued to motivate me.

Thanks to all the authors (my colleagues and friends) for their contributions and support. Thanks are due to all researchers whose works have informed our writings, and our respondents for openly sharing their time, experiences and information with us.

Our publishers have joined us because of their belief in research, and have helped us in sharing our work with a wider audience. We gratefully acknowledge their support and goodwill.

Last but not the least thanks are due to my loving family.

R.G. Dastidar

Contents

The Contributors

Chaudhary, Pratima. is a faculty in the Department of Distance and Continuing Education in Barkatullah University.

Chima, Harneet is Reader in the Department of Sociology, Sarojini Naidu Government Girls College, Bhopal.

Dastidar, Ruchi G., Reader, Department of Sociology and Social Work, Barkatullah University, Bhopal.

Kashyap, Kumaresh S., Reader, Department of Sociology and Social Work, Barkatullah University, Bhopal.

Mohanty, Tapan is Reader in Sociology, National Law Institute University, Bhopal.

Sanyal, Meghna is teaching Sociology in the Department of Sociology, Hari Singh Gaur University, Sagar and is also actively pursuing her doctoral work.

Sharma, Namrata, Reader, Academic Staff College, Devi Ahilya Bai University, Indore.

Sharma, Shrinath, Professor, Department of Sociology, Hari Singh Gaur University, Sagar.

Introduction

Ruchi G. Dastidar

> "We can only act in our own times, and among the people who surround us"
>
> *Albert Camus*

Phoolan Devi became the face of female criminality and shook the society by her extent of and capacity for violence. She was not the first or the last woman criminal but has had predecessors and successors both. Recent years have seen Tarannum, Santokeben, etc. On the other hand stories of violence against women of all ages have found new heights and can be seen to be globally pervasive.

The present volume tries to explore some of the aspect of crime and women within a gendered framework. Articles on crime against women and crime committed by women are together for they both show the vulnerability of women's lives. The final outcome of crime is the destruction of women's life and also womanhood. Crime is often used to subordinate and control women, but becoming perpetuators of crime does not automatically free women of such oppression. Living lives of criminals on the contrary often further threatens on the already narrow space allowed to women and they are not able to overcome their gender limitations and destiny. A woman in crime often works with all the gender burden and increased vulnerability. Further research has shown that these seemingly opposite situations may actually be seen related in so far women specific crimes are concerned. Dowry, girl child infanticide, prostitution, etc., are women specific for they reflect the social status of women as a category, a fact borne out in the pattern of crime itself. Also statistics have shown that women criminals in these categories are amongst the highest, which is no coincidence. Why is it that more women criminals happen to be involved in women related crime? The all male cliché that, "women themselves are women's worst enemies" has been seen to be a false statement in the context of gender studies. Women are the product of the times and the social context they live in and cannot be blamed for carrying patriarchal values and preferences as a consequence of their socialization. Considering that even today in India more women are registered under women related crime, speaks for assertions of women as a category with separate identity. To that extent women's criminal statistics tends to reflect on the social structure, and circumstances of women in the choices they make. Naturally today we have more statistics on women and crime due to various reasons, which include better methodological approach as also increased reporting. Thus crime committed by women and crime committed against women tends to be inextricably interrelated. Some of the articles bring out these patterns explicitly.

Besides, the conception of crime has changed. This has impacted women. On the one hand there has been the diffusion of global culture and values along with institutions and systems like the expanding market system. There have also been a breakdown or withdrawal of traditional institutions of social security, while on the other hand there have been introduction of new institutions like the legal system for example. All this has affected the way women relate to society and their accesses to social systems. An increase in the awareness and change in women's rights and roles is being observed. There does seem a keener sense of justice as also increased assertion of rights at some levels. How have these impacted women? Can statistics on crime help us unravel these patterns?

Some cases of tribal women seem to suggest cultural conflict. However, there always are many factors and processes determining individual action, all of which cannot be explored in one volume. Crime is a very complex phenomena and no civilization has found the perfect understanding or the perfect answer to it.Crime continues to evoke a sharp reaction from the society. It is a matter of popular concern. Administrators and rulers have grappled with it since centuries. Crime and criminals is the ultimate test of any society and its social system. Knowing what kind of crimes are committed in any society and how those criminals are treated shows you the stuff that society is made of. Crime is what society permits, barring individual aberrations, because crime is the direct demonstration of how social and individual (group) needs are achieved and social means of achieving them. Societal perceptions of crime address its value system, and demonstrate its lines of power and social structuring. How any society treats its criminals is proof of its sensitivity and priorities. "The perfect crime of our times, are the crime committed by the rich and not the smart, as is usually the perception. If you can buy the system you are as smart as it gets" (Camus: 1951). For, crime is not only about what one does, but it is as much about who does what. Does this hold true for women?

Clearly perception of crime is time, space, group and culture specific. Yet there is no single one world in this sense. How does this local definiteness lead to global indefiniteness? How do local exigencies relate to global ones? Or how do global perceptions, ideals, practices, processes and interests relate to or influence the local and the *vice versa*? Can crime be classified according to social systems? Therefore, what kind of congruence can be seen between social structures and normative systems world over? What do these world systems, of whatever little continuities, achieved? Do they tell a different story about crime and its world? As also about the world fraternity and the chasm between social reality and the ideal.

Looking at the arms, human trafficking or drugs network for instance does show a pattern and global continuities, while dowry may not. At the same time it is also true that women in South Asia are worse than their sisters elsewhere. On the other hand will one globe mean one crime pattern? In that case we are posed to see a rise in women criminal activities for research has shown that crime committed by women in the developed world is higher than that recorded in under-developed countries, India specifically and other developing countries in general.

Crime is thus the interplay of need, lust, power and the social systems and its processes, through which individuals, as much as by groups, and indeed nations, meet these ends. Structural changes in world systems do not annihilate crime, nor does development, as has been well borne out by centuries of human history. Crime is endemic and the system itself. Organized crime and crime committed by people at the helm of affairs are the ones to watch, not only because of its impact on society at large but also because of its sensitivity to social processes. Thus they become useful tools in the hands of sociologist. Some studies have highlighted how crime may have a social purpose for individual as well as society.

Crime is also seen to bring out the complexities of multicultural, diverse and sometimes contradictory social order as much as it exposes the suppressed frustrations of social order itself. Well demonstrated in various studies, notably in Durkheim's study of social control and anomie in various societies as also in his study of suicide. Although crime appears to be an individual's response to his social circumstances, yet it remains in the ultimate analysis, a manifestation of structural and cultural strains. Poverty, patriarchy, gender issues, class, caste, religion, etc., have been shown to be causative factors by various social scientists time and again (Cohen, Merton, Sutherland, Cavanis and Johnson, etc.)

"Values, usually represents a transition from facts to rights, from what is desired to what is desirable." (Camus :1951). A value transcends the individual and replaces him by the anticipated collectivity. Yet since values are ideational their actual transition may or may not occur, or may differ group to group, or may even have been an illusion of perception. Is the criminal, or any individual for that matter, aware of collective needs? Or does the individual act out of only his need? How does he choose out of the various social alternatives present before him? The available statistics in crime go much beyond limitations of socialization. Crime does happen because of illogical imbalances in our system. It happens because of maladjustments and failure of associated institutions and personnel. Some of it is also freak, but it is also institutional. It is in the world of crime that the lines of power are laid out and consolidated. When groups or individuals outside the institutionalized authority structure get disproportionate power there is an acceleration of criminal activities. Crime is used to legitimize, consolidate, appropriate power. These shifts can hardly be called aberration of the system. It may well be the system itself, therefore, it serves as the indicator of social change. Every social system finds its reflection in the world of crime. Crime is hardly the freak it is made out to be, it actually serves the system (Camus : *ibid*). Richard Quinine argues that, " crime is not inherent in behaviour but is a judgment made by some about the actions of others". How many women criminals fit into this kind of analysis of crime and criminal patterns? Theories in this area have been mostly constructed around power and conflict. An area where women's participation has been traditionally seen to be low. No wonder then most theories on crime tends to ignore women. There is little to go by in trying to understand why women become criminals in the gender sense, more studies focus on the reverse process.

Thus sociological studies in this area have shown how studies in crime can be seen as a critical tool of gauging societies. Mass violence against the weaker sections of society, whether on the basis of class, caste, race or religion, gender frequently forms a pattern. Women are the usual victims. Gang rape of women of the lower caste group, or beating up of women in public places or abusing them is familiar news. Feminists, react very strongly to violence against women. At the theoretical level, however, defining crime has posed various problems. As pointed out earlier crime is time, space and culture specific. What may shock and revolt one society may well be considered only natural in another. *Sati* worship among some Hindus is one such example; and female circumcision is routinely practiced in some African countries. Look at how societies perceive and deal with corruption for instance does it appear to be an issue for most? For the elite?

Crime has also been seen to be garbed as religion or traditions and may be institutionalised. *Sati pratha* or the practice of *devdasi*, for instance. Thugree has been shown to be a religious cult (Bruce : 1969) and there are numerous examples of tribes or endogamous groups living delinquent lives (Kapadia : 1952). Then how does one define crime?

Simply said crime is an act which breaks the law of the land. This is a perspective which is increasingly gaining grounds and to that extent crime is institutionally defined. However, women's role and status remains defined more by tradition, religion and morality and receives sanctions accordingly, sometimes even against the law of the land. Laws then, have to reflect social consensus, concerns, structuring, amongst other things. Clearly the law of any land will have to serve the ruling elite (Mills, Marx, etc.), but even a casual glance will show that not all laws do that. For instance, the human rights movement is definitely non-elitist or democratic to that extent. This ambivalence is often carried in media stories which highlight the atrocities or incapacities of the police. Thus as is obvious, there is a pattern to crime. What do crime stories tell us? What does crime mean to the criminal? How does it relate to and affect different strata's of the population? Do women, aged, children, and weaker sections of society, etc. perceive crime differently? Perception of crime will have ramification on how lives are lived and the social world experienced. Subaltern studies have shown the internalization of elites values to the negation of self-threats, for example, charges of witchcraft occur in a number of Indian States that have large tribal populations with traditional beliefs about witches. Indian newspapers periodically publish reports about women who, after being accused of being witches, have been beaten, had their heads shaved or had strings of shoes hung around their necks. Some have been killed. "Superstition is only an excuse. Often a woman is branded a witch so that you can throw her out of the village and grab her land, or to settle scores, family rivalry, or because powerful men want to punish her for spurning their sexual advances. Sometimes it is used to punish women who question social norms," says Pooja Singhal Purwar, an official at the Jharkhand Social Welfare Department. (*Washington Post*, 8th August,2005).Gender studies too demonstrate the internalization of patriarchy. Does crime then display the existence of an alternative value system, which may exhibit suppressed frustration to open rebellion itself? Are we then on the vortex of social restructuring in the women's question? Adelly (1976) in her *Sisters in Crime* does not think so.

Women have been the subjects of numerous researches. The impetus coming from various international compulsions, social processes and ground realities. Recent years has seen some attention given to women and crime. Studies have explored both, the impact of crime on women's lives as well as the role of women in crime. The former of course dominates our attention for numerous reasons.

Worse still violence seems to be socially sanctioned to some degree, (Kudchedkar and Issa : 1998) although legally it is certainly not ratified. According to National Crimes Report Bureau, 1.5 lakh crimes against women are registered annually out of which nearly 50,000 are related to domestic violence. It is believed that close to 5 crore women suffer from violence in their homes; the feminist movement has very strongly reacted to crime committed against women, and it is increasingly being argued that violence against women is a manifestation of patriarchy. It is the cause of women's subjugation and assertion of male power. Chitnis (1998); Meera Kosambi (1998); etc.

Crime committed by women has not received much attention until recently. Most theoretical formulations tend to see women criminals as an aberration and, therefore, unwomanly; and, therefore, by its very definition there cannot be very many women in crime. Women criminals are hardly a miniscule compared to male criminals and presumably in unwomanly situations, thus not much research has been done in the area. With few theoretical formulations exploring the factors and relationship of women, crime and society, earlier researchers tend to treat women criminals without any gendered theoretical formulations. Social reality, however, calls for gender understanding of female offenders as has been increasingly realized by researches on girl child infanticide or female foeticide for example. Also recent years have seen the involvement of more women in crime, but women criminals remain distinct category *vis-à-vis* men for various reasons, which are predominantly gendered.

In the context of the women's liberation movement it is presumed that the world is becoming more a gendered and that role stereotypes are fast dying out. Given this rise of feminism there should be a loosening of morals and a consequent rise in female criminality. This formulation was explored by Adelly (1976). Recent research in criminology suggests power conflict and gender as explanations of crime. It is also suggested that statistics over represent women in minor crimes due to the insensitivity and bias of the system.

Crime exposes the vulnerability of women to social institutions and processes, and the limitations they face because of social constructs, which are predominantly male. Considering that criminology in the ultimate analysis is the reflection of the working of law agencies, it is imperative that more studies on how women are impacted by it are done. In a global world the formal institutions of social control and, therefore, social structuring will have a greater role to play, it is thus required that these agencies are strengthened and strictly monitored. Crime and women is a direct reflection of the status of women in society. If we want greater adherence to human rights and want women to play a greater role in society, criminology and women can well serve as a critical tool.

Madhya Pradesh is seen as one of the four laggard States in so far as women are concerned. Demographic statistics paint a sorry picture along most indices of social status and development. Worse still Madhya Pradesh is the highest on record in crime against women. Mostly it is a State of dichotomies as the modern gets juxtaposed along with the traditional. With a sizeable population of SC/ST, yawning problems of development and still a strongly feudal society Madhya Pradesh has a somewhat different story to tell. Incidentally data on crime committed by women is not available as official statistics nor is it tabulated head-wise that is reflective of popular perception of the problem. More visibility is accorded to crime committed against women.

The first article by Prof. Sharma explores the perception of women and crime in the cultural and historic context, and sees women as social victims and not free arbitrators of crime. Dr. Kashyap looks at the social and cultural factors which impact crime one way or the other and questions the categorization of crime. Dr. Chima focuses on crime committed against women and surprises by her collection of world patterns and practices. Dr. Mohanty work starts from the theoretical journey of crime and women and goes on to discuss the judicial response to crime against women. Dr Chaudhary's research on Domestic violence in Bhopal is presented as a short paper here and highlights the impact of such situations on the victim and family and offers some suggestions for coping. Dr. Sharma's article on girl child infanticide brings out the extent of the problem in Madhya Pradesh. The last article is about women prisoners in

Bhopal central jail and reflects on their experiences and problems there in the gendered framework.

References

Adler, Freda (1976): *The Rise of the New Female Criminal.* McGraw-Hill, New York.

Ahuja, Ram (1996): *Sociological Criminology*, New Age International Publishers, New Delhi.

Altekar, A.S. (1956) : *The Position of Women in Hindu Civilization*, Motilal Banarsi Das, Benaras.

Bhushan, Vidya (1970) : *Prison Administration in India, with special reference to Uttar Pradesh*. S Chand & Co., New Delhi.

Bottoms, A. (1996):Sexism and Female Offender, Grower Publishing, Sydney.

Braye, Kerryhttp://www.keltawebconcepts.com.au

Brown, B. (1986): *Women and Crime : The Dark Figures of Criminology, Economy and Society*, Vol.15.

Bruce, George : (1968) : *The Stranglers, the Cult of Thuggee and its overthrow in British India*. Harcourt Brace and World Inc., New York.

Camus, A. (1951) : *The Rebel*, Knopf Publishers.

Chaudhuri, A.B. (1984.) : *Witch Killings amongst Santhals*. Ashish Pub. House, New Delhi.

Cohen, Albert K. (1955) : *Delinquent Boys : A Culture of the Gang*. Free Press, New York.

Diwan, Paras (1987) : *Dowry and Protection to Married Women*. Deep & Deep Pub., New Delhi.

Feinman, C. (1994) : *Women in the Criminal Justice Systems*. Praeger Publishers, West Port

Glesthorpe and Morris (ed.) (1990) : *Feminist Perspectives in Criminology*. Open University Press, London.

Haikerwal, B.S. : *Economic and Social Aspects of Crime in India*. George Allen and Unwin Ltd., London, 1934.

Kapadia, K .M.(1952) : "The Criminal Tribes of India" in *Sociological Bulletin,* I,11March .

Marcus-Mendza : (2004) : *Feminist Therapy Behind Bars*, Feminist Press at the City University, New York.

Merton, R.K. (1967) : *Social Theory and Social Structure*. Free Press, New York.

Miller, W.B.: "Lower Class Culture as a Generating Milieu of Gang Delinquency" in *Journal of Social Issues*, vol. 14, no. 3

Naffine, N. (1997) : *Feminism and Criminology*. Allen and Unwin, Sydney.

Nayar, Baldev Raj (1975) : *Violence and Crime In India: A Quantitative Study*. Macmillan India Ltd., Delhi. .

Reid, Sue Titus (1976): *Crime and Criminology*, The Drydon Press, Illinois.

Vold, George B. (1958) : *Theoretical Criminology*. Oxford University Press, New York..

1
Women and Crime

Srinath Sharma

Women and crime are often used synonymously and their relationship is very old. Their existence in the society is not as old as the social concepts of gender inequality, leadership friendship and conflict. The nexus between women and crime emerged due to the establishment of a patriarchal society. Many anthropological thinkers believe that "Women occupied a central place in all state of affairs during the preliminary period of social evolution". The dominance of men over women took fine shape with progression of society for which thinkers like E.B. Tylor[1] and Bachofen[2] have provided different views.

The Greek and Indian literature provides various instances of women discussing and going against the social norms. The famous Greek example is that of Venus. The era of Vedic and Post Vedic India reflects punishment given to women, (for example Sita, Vrinda and Ahilya) for committing crimes, which can no longer be considered as crimes in today's society. But dwelling deep into dark caves of history to find out the nexus between women and crime will lead to no solution rather reflection on the status of women in the middle ages is necessary whose historical significance is unquestionable. Before starting any discussions it would be relevant to clarify about our questions and limitations of discussion.

Discussions on the subject of women and crimes based on

the hypothesis that powerful classes in the society have always considered the voice of the weaker sections as crime. Punishing women reflects the dominance of one group over the other. Women are considered as weak, fragile and delicate in this middle age and cruel era. In the present society men are taking benefit of this concept and forcing women in the world of crime. Through this article we would try to present sociological analysis of increasing correlations between women and crime.

Many women during the middle age became popular because of breaking 'social norms', which was considered crime and were thus punished. For example, Mirabai, a Rajput princess of 15th century raised her voice against conventional customs for which she was forced to drink poison as a punishment. In the same period another well known Bengali woman named "Rami" married to "Chandi Das" a Vaishnav poet belonging to different caste.[3] Janabai born in *Shudra caste* family of Maharashtra fought against the social harassment by becoming devotee of God.[4] Mahadevi Akka and Sule Sunkawa of Karnataka belonging to *Veer Shiva* sect became famous in 12th Century for raising voices against orthodox customs.[5] Mahadevi Akka worshipped Lord Shiva remaining nude and Sule Sunkawa embraced social harassment by practicing prostitution and worshipping Lord Shiva.[6] Chandrobati author of Bengali *Ramayana* portrayed Goddess Sita as a courageous and self-respected woman as against Lord Rama who was considered a weak husband, fearful son and unsuccessful king during his reign[7]. Chandrobati did not believe in the institution of marriage and rebelled unfavourable laws formulated for penalizing women in society. The work of Chandrobati is an anecdote of courage for not paying taxes in the reign of Allauddin Khilji, Sultan of Delhi may be a remarkable example of appreciation but these examples quoted above have been considered as crime. The list of women involved directly or indirectly in committing crimes during the middle ages were only few.

Women across the country in the States of Gujarat,

Maharashtra, West Bengal and South India were actively involved in raising voice against the social norms and male dominated society. Scattered social movements could not prove to be helpful in inculcating feelings in favour of women, which formed the basis of these movements. Thus the status of women in India was encompassed as a symbol of forgiveness, love, and motherhood, and proved instrumental in defining two functional roles played by women. On the one hand she is an individual full of emotions while on the other hand women are vulnerable and subjected to violence without retaliating in return. These notions and beliefs are not born all of a sudden but are the result of latent and unconscious social progress.

Since long the personality traits reflected by both men and women are divided according to the automotory nervous system. A child cries for its mother when injured or is in pain and remembers father if scared or finds some event to be fearful. These illustrations explain that motherhood of a woman relates itself to be subjected to any kind of violence while men are symbols of scaring others or symbols of masculinity is symbolic of fighting fear.

Effects of collective consciousness over individual consciousness have been dealt in detail by eminent social scientists Emile Durkheim through various illustrations.[8] This collective and conscious structure has dominated superstructure of our conscious mind. Many notions and concepts could be established due to the conflicts and adjustment between individual's consciousness and collective consciousness. For instance women are less attracted towards committing any crime. They want to stay away from any crime and they knowingly give less priority to crime and violence.

An idea that "Benefits of various movements and technological innovations would be reaped by opportunists and those into power if change is not acceptable by the society",[9] is accorded a status of principle nowadays. If we provide affiliation to the above idea then it is clearly evident that criminals have utilized the benefits of non-criminal image of women. Some crimes where it is impossible to believe that women could be used, underworld dons and con-men have utilized and exploited women to their fullest.

When we have reached to this point let us know that the nexus between women and criminals is not a product of this modern world. Historical evidence prove that Kautilya has sent woman (*Vish Kanya*) to the palace of King Parvatraj[10] and women spy were sent to places like *antahpur* or *ranivas* for conspiracy work.

Dr. Ram Manohar Lohia once made a comparison between princess Padmini (famous for *johar*) of Chittorgarh and Natali (German spy during World War-II). Natali who learned the techniques of war and passed it to the German soldiers during World War-II was praised worthy[11].

Men are found to be responsible for including women in different criminal activities varying from crimes done for the welfare of the nation in the past, for selling drugs, using them as sharp shooters or forcefully involving women in prostitution in the present days. Men are getting benefits either directly or indirectly through the involvement of women in various crimes. Notion of women don has also been realized and more and more women today are committing crime for fulfilling their desires and have been symbolized as men by different thinkers. For example in his book *Stri Ke Liye Jagah* (space for women) Raj Kishore through his articles has emphasized that women who have established themselves are found to be in accordance with men's role[12]. But this fact describes the collective consciousness of our society, which is not in favour of seeing women outside the boundary of love, care and motherhood.

Women are also found to be involved in another kind of crime apart from non–traditional and hardcore crime. For example, burning brides for dowry, women exploitation through remarriage by men without divorce forcing daughter or daughter-in-law for prostitution. If data related to such crime is gathered and analysed then women would be found involved in both sides of criminal process that is, as a victim as well as a criminal. This factual evidence is in conflict of our hypothesis. But we have to see that values used as inspiration for committing crimes are established by male dominated society and thus ultimately are profitable for men. Thus men are being benefited only by crimes committed by women against women. Like husband being benefited through remarriage after daughter-in-law is burnt alive by mother-in-law, as in some cases establishing business of sons by selling daughter/ daughter-in-law.

When entire scenario is present wearing different shades of modernism and start presenting some kind of logical inference then it should be analyzed by post-modernism thoughts of "Nitze" which he has propounded addressing morality of slaves.[13] Accordingly women who commit crime against women and accept it as a social pattern are justifying themselves as "Slaves of Illogical Morality".

The Post Modern Turn written by Ehab Hussain[14] clearly depicts the dominance of post modernism on changing scenario of "Art and Literature" and "Cinema and Media". The literature widely written and published on the "Liberation Movements for Women" has not been able to influence as much as the marketing of literature written and published on "Deconstruction of Status of Women as a Value of Post Modernism".

The Hindi literature once gave more fame to Gulshan Nanda than to *Muktiboudh*. The current scenario of literature shows the same trend. Today, people are more interested to read books and novels of Shobha De or James Hadley as against Geirman Grear or *French-the Byowar* written on women liberation. Taking a sharp look at the media projection will reveal that Kalpna Azmi is less renowned than the producers like Ekta Kapoor and Pooja Bhatt showing women to be valueless identity.

The above discussion can be depicted more clearly through a diagram.

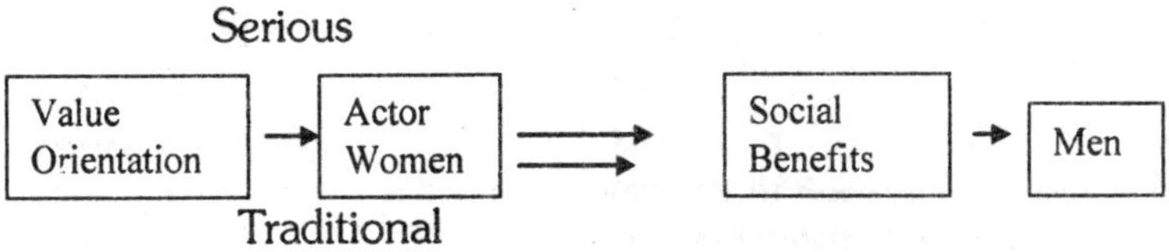

The diagram shows that an individual born in a society gets more influenced by the customs, values and inspirations in the social action. Supporting the theory reflects that women engaged in different forms of crime is a result of social values and social orientation. Development of such values and orientation is a result of the invisible web of superstructure laid down by the male dominated society. A woman thus fall prey to that particular web and fails to understand that the crime in which she would be engaged would directly or indirectly yield benefits either to males or to male dominated society at her cost.

Theories and ideologies of structuralism and neo-structuralism could be verified through nexus of women and crime. A.R. Radcliffe Brown believed that actions performed by actors or changes arrived at in social institutions through incoming or outgoing of individuals could eradicate social static but could not induce social revolution because factual social relationships do not change.[15] Alike Brown, famous American sociologist Talcott Parsons in his AGIL model (adaptation, goal attainment, integration and latency) describes latency in a similar fashion.

The above analysis does not illustrate the nexus between women and crime empirically rather it reflects on the illegitimate involvement of women in crime and gives rise to another question as to why women are involving themselves in such violent crimes?

Whether a woman is the slave of man or not, she remains

so, at least in the partial sense of the term. Even when she is shunned to some dark corner of society not even affected by the rays of the sun. It is well established that even in societies, which provide legal liberation to women, there too women are not allowed to take fundamental decisions. When women are not allowed to take their own decisions whether positive or negative then freedom related to criminal decisions made by them would remain questionable.

Notes

1. Tylor, E.B.: *Religion in Primitive Cultures*, Harpper Torch Books, New York, 1958.
2. Bachofen: Quoted in *An Introduction to Anthropological Thought*, Vikas Publications, Ranchi, 1983, p.33.
3. Mehrotra, D.P. : *Bhartiya Mahila Andolan*, Books For Change, New Delhi, 2003, p.26-27.
4. *Ibid.*, p.16.
5. *Ibid.*, p.17
6. *Ibid.*, p.18.
7. *Ibid.*
8. Durkheim, E. : Quoted in *Main Currents in Sociological Thoughts*, Raymond Aron.
9. Rajkishore : *Stri Ke Liye Jagah*, Vani Prakashan, New Delhi,1996, Editorial.
10. Bais, Ishwar Singh : "Aourat Adami Itihas ke Aine Main"; *Saptahik Hindustan*, August 1973, p. 33.
11. Lohia, Ram Manohar : *Padmini or Natali*, Jan Navhind Prakashan, Hyderabad, 1966.
12. Rajkishore : *Stri Ke Liye Jagah*, *op. cit.*
13. Nitze: Quoted by Manager Pandey in "Uttar Audhunikata Ke Dhol Ki Pole", *Jansatta*, 12th Dec. 1997, New Delhi.
14. Hasan, Ihab : quoted by Ramesh Upadhyaya, " Aaj Ka Punjivad Aur Uska Uttar Audhunikatavad" in *Man Dand*, R.C. Shukla, Shodh Sansthan, Varanasi, 1997, pp.94-95.
15. Radcliff-Brown, A.R. : "Structure and function in Primitive Society", Routledge and Kegan Paul, London, 1979.

2
Structural and Institutional aspect of Crime against Women

Kumaresh S. Kashyap

Introduction

Globally women are a disadvantaged group although they constitute over 50 per cent of the world's population. Women owe just one per cent of the world's property and resources, perform 60 per cent of the labour, and account for the majority of refugees, illiterate and poor in the world. Violence against women is a pandemic that knows no boundaries of culture, geography, age or wealth. Yet, the public generally downplays it as social processes and continue to support men's societal dominance. Interestingly, the actors were once children simulating the perpetuation of violence through familiar but sick themes of bride price, female infanticide and privileging the son at the expense of the daughter, etc.

Feminist scholars contend that domestic violence is rooted in gender and power and represents men's active attempts to maintain dominance and control over women. The cultural depiction of the husband as the breadwinner has legitimized male power within the family. It provides men with a resource for demonstrating their masculinity. But when their masculinity is challenged, then violence is a culturally appropriate means to exert dominance and control. While factors such as low income, unemployment and age affect the perpetration of domestic assaults by men, the violence is by no means confined to the lower economic strata of society. The importance of the patriarchal social structure in the dictionary of domestic violence cannot be overstated. Hence, the discrimination against and abuse of women is hardly uncommon within affluent or well-educated families.

The abuse of women stems from a multiplicity of cultural circumstances influenced by power relations. Violence is rooted in structural inequality and becomes an ultimate resource used to derive power within relationships. Women play a central role as subsistence producers and providers of basic needs in diverse countries but they continue to be underrepresented in positions of power. Existing inequalities between men and women are reinforced by policies. Women have been the main agents of the remarkable change in the attitudes and understanding that has occurred; that acts of domestic violence can no longer be marginalized as personal tragedies. Feminists and activists have brought acts of domestic violence out of the private sphere and into the public realm so that the personal has become political.

Violence against women is a complex issue as it is rooted in masculinity structures of power. But more and more people are beginning to realize that violence against women is not 'normal'; more women are coming forward to report crimes against them; more women realize that they are not to blame for the rapes or assaults they have suffered; more women have begun to demand justice. This is empowerment; it is slow progress but it is still progressing. Not that there have been no efforts in the past to contain the rising violence against women. The Dowry Prohibition Act 1961 has been amended twice to make its provisions more stringent and punitive. The Indian Penal Code, the Criminal Procedure Code and the Indian Evidence Act have also been changed simultaneously to deal effectively with not only dowry deaths but also the cases of cruelty to married women. Similarly, suitable modifications in the law against rape have been incorporated to remove some of its drawbacks. But all these changes have not reduced the frequency of crime at all.

Objectives of preventive laws may not be faulted, but what is of crucial importance is their enforcement. A wide gap exists between laws with high social and economic purposes and their implementation on account of police inefficiency and widespread corruption all around. In this climate, the cutting edge of laws, both as an instrument of crime prevention and of social change, should be bound to get blunted. The position further gets aggravated when the populace flouting, perverting or getting round the letter and spirit of the law sees the culprits. So long as these laws are not accompanied by the empowerment of women at all levels and a sense of accountability in the enforcing agency, they will serve little purpose. In any case, legal remedies alone cannot cope with a regressive socio-economic set-up in the absence of radical, structural and economic reforms, which can be implemented only by mass mobilization and participation. But with the kind of bureaucracy, police and political set-up that we have, the mere passing of laws will not serve any purpose.

More important than legislative reforms is the strict enforcement of rights already available to women in relation to property matters. In fact, women's plight is compounded by their reluctance to seek legal remedies even if they are aware of them. The voluntary surrender of their rights in the matter of inheritance is the single biggest reason why women suffer the disgrace of dowry that continues to make marriage an ordeal or a death trap for many of them. In realistic sense, the problem of violence against women has its roots in a socio-economic order that is heavily biased against women. The ancient law books, in effect, equate women with beasts and drums meaning that like the latter two, women also deserve to be beaten. A woman in revolt, a woman having an identity of her own, is a concept totally alien to Indian culture.

When the entire milieu is steeped overwhelmingly in the tradition of women's utter subjection to men, when the belief continues to persist that women are mere property to be procured and dispensed with in the service of the male, there can be little hope for a dramatic uplift in the state of women. Only a change in this fundamental perception to one of according women total equality in all things can bring about the radical transformation in society where crime will not be committed against them merely because they are women.

Caste Structure and Gender Bias

In every part of the world, women's roles and positions in society are prescribed. One of the key aspects of every culture is the way it defines gender roles. Almost without exception women are assigned to roles that are subservient to those of men. Virtually every culture in the world contains forms of violence against women that are nearly invisible because they are seen as "normal" and has cultural sanction supporting men at large. Gender refers to the attributes associated with being male and female. Rather than being biologically determined, gender is a set of learned behaviours, shaped by expectations that stem from the idea that certain qualities, behaviours, characteristics, needs and roles are "natural" and desirable for men, while others are "natural" and desirable for women. Gender is a critical element of power and inequality. Women's gender roles are generally accorded less political, economic, social and cultural value than those of men. Even in countries where laws criminalize violence against women, tolerance of violence may be found at all levels of society. The lacks of political will to eradicate violence can be seen, for example, in the failure to establish and fund programmes to educate the population, to train government employees and to support measures to protect victims of violence.

Often, the behaviour of a woman is considered to reflect on her family and community. If a woman is seen to be defying her cultural role, she may be held to have brought shame and dishonour on her family and community. In such circumstances, violence or the threat of violence is used as a means of punishment and control.

In the most extreme cases, this can result in permanent disfigurement and even death. So called "honour" crimes are treated leniently in the legal codes of many countries. Community values may foster or facilitate violence against women. Women themselves are sometimes complicit in perpetrating violence against other women. Cultural stereotypes are often used to justify abuses against women from specific racial, national and religious groups. The common practice of denying women equal rights to property and inheritance exacerbates their subordinate and dependent status. Not only are women denied these economic rights, they are often considered to be the property of their fathers or husbands- as tradeable commodities. Victims of violence from marginalized and low income communities are often denied the level of support that woman from wealthier or politically elite communities receive.

Article 1 UN Convention on the Elimination of All Forms of Discrimination Against Women (CEDAW) of the Convention against Torture states: "For the purposes of this Convention, the term 'torture' means any act by which severe pain or suffering, whether physical or mental, is intentionally inflicted on a person for such purposes as obtaining from him or a third person information or a confession, punishing him for an act he or a third person has committed or is suspected of having committed, or intimidating or coercing him or a third person, or for any reason based on discrimination of any kind, when such pain or suffering is inflicted by or at the instigation of or with the consent or acquiescence of a public official or other person acting in an official capacity. It does not include pain or suffering arising only from, inherent in or incidental to lawful sanctions."

Article 1 of the UN Convention on the Elimination of All Forms of Discrimination Against Women (CEDAW) against Torture defines state responsibility for acts of torture and ill treatment by private individuals (such as abusive husbands or other family members) if carried out with the "consent or acquiescence of a public official". Human rights experts have pointed out that all the elements of torture can be present in domestic violence (violence in the family). It may cause severe physical and mental pain, and may be intentionally inflicted for a specific purpose. If a state tacitly condones domestic violence by not exercising due diligence and equal protection in preventing and punishing it, then it bears responsibility for the abuses.

Socialization and Status of Women

The fisherwomen especially in rural areas have remained backward for long due to various socio-economic constraints. These constraints emerge from illiteracy, traditional values and norms, dominant positions of males, superstition, economic dependence of women on men, social evils like dowry and polygamy, low work participation and discrimination. Though women have been denied equal opportunities all over the world for personal growth and social development in India the situation is still worse because of the sex segregated characters of society, poverty and traditional values (Grappa, 1994). Thus it is obvious that the status role of fisherwomen is different from that of other women owing to different social stratification existing in their surrounding areas. They seems obvious from the relevant data gathered from the villages under study.

The problem of women development varies according to the given situation. Unlike in agriculture or household work, women participation in fisheries is subjected to many peculiarities. Where a particular activity signifies a major role for women like fish marketing, the influence of men over them may be found. When both men and women have equal role in certain activities like fish rearing women may be relegated to traditional method or simpler jobs rather than modern methods. According to the interviewed women the emancipation of women is still increasing and specially differences in participation in marketing and decision-making is getting smaller. Of the women respondents engaged in fishing 80 per cent are full timers and 20 per cent are part-timers. Majority has education up to primary or slightly above primary level and may also be illiterate. In these surveys only one girl has been reported to reach the level of graduation.

India has traditionally been a male society. There is a strong preference to son in most parts of India, and girls tend to be discriminated against by their families. It is not enough, therefore, to highlight adolescence in general; a larger focus of the girl child also must be addressed. Demographic trends indicate deep rooted gender discrimination Discrimination begins with female foeticide and prenatal sex determination.

Girls are deprived of nutrition, access to health care, and opportunities for education and employment. They are taken out of schools when they reach menarche. From the very beginning of life, girls are groomed to accommodate the male-dominated, patriarchal society. Girl children grow into adulthood without being able to experience the important period of adolescence. They work in the home, look after siblings, and assist their mothers in the fields. Then they are married off early to soon become mothers themselves, still unarmed with knowledge about reproductive needs and rights. The situation is similar, more or less, in different States of the country.

Why did a fairly large number of adolescent girls not attend schools? More than one-quarter of girls' lack of education was ascribed to their responsibilities for caring for siblings at home and other household work and the social context and gender socialization that set girls and boys on separate lifetime paths in terms of life expectations, educational attainment, job prospects, labour force participation, reproduction, and duties in the household. The report also outlines laws and policies that pertain to and discusses information and service delivery programmes that provide reproductive health information and services to adolescents. However, despite adolescents being a huge segment of the population, policies and programmes in India have focused very little effort on the adolescent group. Over the past 50 years, the population has grown at a rapid pace and so, too, has the adolescent population, despite a formal and a well-organized family planning programme in India.

Until quite recently, the approach of the family planning programme has focused on achieving demographic goals by increasing contraceptive use. The commitment of the national government to the reproductive health approach forged at the International Conference on Population and Development (ICPD) in 1994 has reshaped the family welfare programme into a broad-based Reproductive and Child Health (RCH) Services Programme in India. Policy-makers and planners have now realized that the adolescent population group has specific health and developmental needs. There is a growing understanding that adolescence is a bridge between childhood and adulthood. The newer focus on RCH also has been invigorated by the continuing realization of the importance of women's health; it is now widely accepted that if the health of women is to be improved, the health of adolescents must be given high priority in Indian policy and programme development and implementation. Unfortunately, the special needs of adolescents are rarely addressed by the educational, health, and family welfare programmes in India.

Adolescence is a transition phase through which a child becomes an adult. It is the period during which rapid physical growth, physiological and psychosocial changes, the development of secondary sexual characteristics, and reproductive maturation occur. During adolescence, an intense sexual drive develops and adolescents typically start exploring relationships with the opposite sex. Adolescents start defining social relationships outside of the family. Their behaviour is guided by an intense desire for independence and identity. In the process, adolescents undergo intense psychological stress and personality change. Male dominance results in preference for son and natural discrimination to women or girl child. Hence adolescence along with girl child needs to be addressed.

The root cause to gender discrimination begins with prenatal sex determination and female Foeticide. Sex pre-selection is popular in many States in India, namely Maharashtra, Rajasthan, Punjab, Haryana, and Tamil Nadu. Why did a fairly large number of adolescent girls not attend schools? More than one-quarter of girls' lack of education was ascribed to their responsibilities for caring for siblings at home and other household responsibilities. Another quarter was ascribed to the cost of education. Among the boys, the main reasons identified for not attending school were a lack of interest in studies and the cost of education. Indian culture promotes universal marriage. Of importance is the traditional young marriage age of girl referred to as early marriage. The national average age at marriage for women in India is 16.4 years, although there are vast regional variations. Most northern and northeastern States, as well as Tamil Nadu and Kerala in the south and Goa in the west, have a higher age at marriage, ranging from age 18 to 22 years. The majority of the States in the western, central, and eastern parts of India reported an average age at marriage similar to the national average.

Adolescents constitute perhaps the healthiest group in the population, having the lowest mortality and morbidity compared with other population age groups. However, the period of adolescence, beginning with the onset of puberty, is a crucial transition into adulthood. Most adolescents go through adolescence with little or no knowledge of the body's impending physical and physiological changes. In a country like India, where discussion about sexuality with young children is almost absent, adolescents are not prepared mentally or psychologically to cope with these changes. During the transition to adulthood, lack of knowledge and awareness about reproductive organs, physiological changes, or sexuality can promote psychosocial stress. This is particularly so for girls, who also face gender discrimination. Adolescent girls and boys experience psychosocial stress. A study conducted by the State Education Resource Centre (SERC) in Uttar Pradesh established that gender equality was unknown and adolescent girls felt that they were a burden on their families and had poorer self-image while their counterparts felt superior.[15] A recent study revealed that 14 per cent of boys and 8 per cent of girls had trouble with sexual thoughts, and nearly 9 per cent of the boys and girls perceived premarital stress.

This is particularly true for girls given that the majority of them have no knowledge of menstruation. In most cases, their mothers are the only source of information. Most girls perceive menstruation as disgusting and as a curse. Adolescent girls are also at higher risk of psychosocial stress because of gender discrimination. There is a lack of knowledge and awareness among adolescents about health issues and problems. An Indian Council of Medical Research (ICMR) study showed that knowledge and awareness about puberty, menstruation, physical changes in the body, reproduction, contraception, pregnancy, childbearing, reproductive tract infections, Sexually Transmitted Infections (STIs), and HIV was low among boys and girls, especially in younger adolescents (aged 10–14 years). Among the younger adolescents, 40 per cent had little knowledge about the sex organs and most girls had not been informed about menarche prior to its onset. About one-half of the adolescents were not aware of condoms and were confused about the various modes of HIV/AIDS transmission. The study reported, however, that older adolescents (aged 15–19 years) had better knowledge. About 80 per cent had knowledge of STIs, including HIV. Older adolescent girls were more aware than younger adolescent girls of the physical and physiological changes that take place in the body. Only one-half of the adolescents were aware of various family planning methods, and young people's knowledge about spacing methods, such as through the use of Intra Uterine Devices (IUDs) or oral contraceptive pills, was very low. High fertility rates, high rates of teenage pregnancy, high risk of STI/HIV, and poor nutritional status are the main health problems among the adolescent population in India. High fertility is related to early marriage.

The Age-Specific Fertility Rate (ASFR) among 15–19 years-old female adolescents is as high as teenage pregnancy, almost all of which takes place within marriage, is the major cause of poor reproductive health and health outcomes among adolescents. About 15 per cent of pregnancies are among teenage girls under 18 years who have a two to five times higher risk of maternal death. Adolescent pregnant mothers, who are often already poorly nourished before becoming pregnant, run a high obstetric risk for premature delivery, giving birth to a low birth weight baby, prolonged and obstructed labour, and severe intrapartum and postpartum haemorrhage. Induced abortions are yet another important reason for the poor reproductive health of women in general and adolescents specifically. An estimated six million induced abortions are performed in India, and anecdotal evidence suggests that a fairly large proportion of them are performed for adolescent mothers and unmarried teenage girls. While no realistic or accurate data are available, the enormity of the problem may be judged by the fact that 8–10 per cent of those who seek medical terminations of pregnancy are teenage mothers and unmarried girls. The real percentage may be far larger. While induced abortion was legalized in India under the Medical Termination of Pregnancy (MTP) Act, a major proportion (approximately 80 per cent) of all induced abortions are still performed illegally by private and untrained persons in unhygienic conditions. Induced abortions account for more than 11 per cent of maternal deaths and significantly influence women's reproductive health.

A large proportion of adolescent girls suffer from various gynaecological problems, there are several gynaecological problems among female adolescents. These problems arise primarily as a result of changing hormone patterns. Anaemia is a widely prevalent health problem among adolescent girls. Adolescence is shrouded in myths and misconceptions about sexual health and sexuality. In Indian culture, talking about sex is taboo. Consequently, little information is provided to adolescents about sexual health. Instead, young people learn more about sexual and reproductive health from uninformed sources, which results in the perpetuation of myths and misconceptions about puberty, menstruation, secondary sex characteristics, physiological and body changes, masturbation, night emissions, sexual intercourse, and STIs.

Value System and Inherent Deviance

There are several barriers to ARH (Adolescent Reproductive Health) in India. The reproductive health needs of adolescents differ according to age, socio-cultural environment, and marital status. Some of these barriers are the following :

- Young and growing children have poor knowledge and lack of awareness about physical and physiological changes associated with the onset and presence of adolescence. They learn about sexuality and secondary sex characteristics primarily from their peer groups or other, inappropriate sources. Most girls are not informed about menarche and how to manage menstrual bleeding, and adolescents also lack knowledge about reproductive health issues. These situations could largely be remedied by effective implementation of school health programmes.
- Married adolescents are more vulnerable because of the serious reproductive health risks associated with early marriage, early sexual activity, and early child bearing. Very few programmes have been able to distinguish between the special reproductive health needs of married and unmarried adolescents.
- In Indian culture, it is not socially acceptable for parents to talk with children about sexuality and reproductive changes. Parents, who could or should be the major

source of information and preparation for the transition into adulthood, have largely been uninvolved with educating their children. In most cases, mothers do not even talk to their daughters about menstruation. To encourage parents to take on this role, there needs to be a focus on increasing awareness and strengthening the environment in which this becomes acceptable behaviour.

- There is a lack of proper information about programmes and availability of services provided by the public sector and NGOs. Information, Education, and Communication (IEC) activities are poorly planned and managed.
- Adolescent health is not a mainstream strategic component of health care in India. Of late, adolescent health has been included as a component of the reproductive health package in the RCH Services Programme. However, there is no clear definition of a strategic approach and activities to provide adolescent health care.
- Access and availability of public health care services are severely limited in general and in particular so for adolescent populations, given their specific health and psychosocial needs.
- Poor counselling skills and services are the major constraints to improved ARH. Health care providers have not received any training in sexuality and reproductive health counselling and are not sensitized to adolescent health needs. Counselling services hardly exist.
- Poor implementation of programmes and special schemes in various sectors can be attributed to a lack of identification of clearly defined objectives, a lack of clearly outlined action plans, a lack of coordination, and a lack of project monitoring processes.

- Programmes are not being sustained. NGO programmes implemented are for a limited period of time and depend on the availability of funds. In the public sector, too, the State Government depends on the Central Government for funds. Funds flow irregularly and are often delayed. Lessons learned are rarely shared and efforts to sustain programming are rarely given serious thought [GoI, (2001)].

Looking through the lens of hunger and poverty, there are seven major areas of discrimination against women in India :

- *Malnutrition :* India has exceptionally high rates of child malnutrition, because tradition in India requires that women eat last and least throughout their lives, even when pregnant and lactating. Malnourished women give birth to malnourished children, perpetuating the cycle.
- *Poor Health :* Females receive less health care than males. Many women die in childbirth of easily prevented complications. Working conditions and environmental pollution further impairs women's health.
- *Lack of education :* Families are far less likely to educate girls than boys, and far more likely to pull them out of school, either to help out at home or from fear of violence.
- *Overwork :* Women work longer hours and their work is more arduous than men's, yet their work is unrecognized. Men report that "women, like children, eat and do nothing." Technological progress in agriculture has had a negative impact on women.
- *Unskilled :* In women's primary employment sector— agriculture — extension services overlook women.

- *Mistreatment :* In recent years, there has been an alarming rise in atrocities against women in India, in terms of rapes, assaults and dowry-related murders. Fear of violence suppresses the aspirations of all women. Female infanticide and sex-selective abortions are additional forms of violence that reflect the devaluing of females in Indian society. Omveat Gail (1990).
- *Powerlessness :* While women are guaranteed equality under the Constitution, legal protection has little effect in the face of prevailing patriarchal traditions. Women lack power to decide whom they will marry, and are often married ofı as children. Legal loopholes are used to deny women inheritance rights.

The Constitution of India grants women equal rights with men, but strong patriarchal traditions persist, with women's lives shaped by customs that are centuries old. In most Indian families, a daughter is viewed as a liability, and she is conditioned to believe that she is inferior and subordinate to men. Sons are idolized and celebrated. *May you be the mother of a hundred sons* is a common Hindu wedding blessing. The origin of the Indian idea of appropriate female behaviour can be traced to the rules laid down by Manu in 200 B.C.: "by a young girl, by a young woman, or even by an aged one, nothing must be done independently, even in her own house. In childhood a female must be subject to her father, in youth to her husband, when her lord is dead to her sons; a woman must never be independent".

The practice of breast-feeding female children for shorter periods of time reflects the strong desire for sons. If women are particularly anxious to have a male child, they may deliberately try to become pregnant again as soon as possible after a female is born. Conversely, women may consciously seek to avoid another pregnancy after the birth of a male child in order to give maximum attention to the new son. A primary way that parents discriminate against their girl children is through neglect during illness. When sick, little girls are not taken to the doctor as frequently as are their brothers. A study in Punjab shows that medical expenditures for boys are 2.3 times higher than for girls.

As adults, women get less health care than men. They tend to be less likely to admit that they are sick and they will wait until their sickness has progressed before they seek help or help is sought for them. Studies on attendance at rural primary health centres reveal that more males than females are treated in almost all parts of the country, with differences greater in northern hospitals than southern ones, pointing to regional differences in the value placed on women. Women's socialization to tolerate suffering and their reluctance to be examined by male personnel are additional constraints in their getting adequate health care.

Working Conditions result in Premature and Still-births *Impact of Pollution on Women*

Work is an important activity where survival comes into foreplay. At the same time in those class where work becomes indispensable at the cost of health is done and it gets influenced to such a limit that the problems generated is considered normal. It is a practice with men folk, hence, sociality inferior category like women at times suffers terribly, and as a result every important stage of life gets influenced. Pregnancy is one of them where the matter is so serious that any lack will certainly influence her and undoubtedly the growing foetus. Pollution remains the factor, which in itself can do less damage but can act as a catalyst to many other problems and can complicate the issue. Women's health is further harmed by air and water pollution and lack of sanitation.

Women and Girls receive far less Education than Men, due both to Social Norms and Fears of Violence

Domestic violence not only disrupts the peace but it ignites the beginning of many activities that may result into the loss of status and identity of being a woman. The primary impact results in loss of identity as being a human. In general enemies are not treated as humans, similarly she loses her right to express in the family, any act person or place is taken to avenging and so this is extended to children and they also suffer the score. Hence, the fear of violence and compulsions of social norms forces her to leave any activity that may pull on the issue and her education is one such example. Women work longer hours and their work is more arduous than men's. Still, men report that "women, like children, eat and do nothing".

The Invisibility of Women's Work

Women's work is rarely recognized. Many maintain that women's economic dependence on men impacts their power within the family. With increased participation in income-earning activities, not only will there be more income for the family, but gender inequality should be reduced. This issue is particularly salient in India because studies show a very low level of female participation in the labour force. This under-reporting is attributed to the frequently held view that women's work is not economically productive.

In a report of the National Commission on Self-Employed Women and Women in the Informal Sector, the Director of Social Welfare in one State said, "There are no women in any unorganized sector in our State." When the Commission probed and asked, "Are there any women who go to the forest to collect firewood? Do any of the women in rural areas have cattle"? the Director responded with, "Of course, there are many women doing that type of work". Working women are invisible to most of the population.

The Impact of Technology on Women

The shift from subsistence to a market economy has a dramatic negative impact on women. Violence against women and girls is the most pervasive human rights violation in the world today. Male violence against women is a worldwide phenomenon. Although not every woman has experienced it, and many expect not to fear of violence is an important factor in the lives of most women. It determines what they do, when they do it, where they do it, and with whom. Fear of violence is a cause of women's lack of participation in activities beyond the home, as well as inside it. Within the home, women and girls may be subjected to physical and sexual abuse as punishment or as culturally justified assaults. These acts shape their attitude to life, and their expectations of themselves.

The insecurity outside the household is today the greatest obstacle in the path of women. Conscious that, compared to the atrocities outside the house, atrocities within the house are endurable, women not only continued to accept their inferiority in the house and society, but even called it sweet.

Selective Abortions

The most extreme expression of the preference for sons is female infanticide and sex-selective abortion. Legal protection of women's rights has little effect in the face of prevailing patriarchal traditions.

Marriage

Women are subordinate in most marriages. Exposure to and

interactions with the outside world are instrumental in determining the possibilities available to women in their daily lives. The situation of women is affected by the degree of their autonomy or capacity to make decisions both inside and outside their own household.

The position of women in northern India is notably poor. Traditional Hindu society in northern rural areas is hierarchical and dominated by men, as evidenced by marriage customs. North Indian Hindus are expected to marry within prescribed boundaries: the bride and groom must not be related, they have no say in the matter, and the man must live outside the woman's natal village.

"Wife givers" are socially and ritually inferior to "wife takers", thus necessitating the provision of a dowry. After marriage, the bride moves in with her husband's family. Such a bride is "a stranger in a strange place". The older females in the household control them, and their behaviour reflects on the honour of their husbands. Because emotional ties between spouses are considered a potential threat to the solidarity of the matrilineal group, the northern system tends to segregate the sexes and limit communication between spouses a circumstance that has direct consequences for family planning and similar "modern" behaviours that affect health. A young Indian bride is brought up to believe that her own wishes and interests are subordinate to those of her husband and his family. The primary duty of a newly married young woman, and virtually her only means of improving her position in the hierarchy of her husband's household, is to bear sons."

Child Marriages

Child marriages keep women subjugated. Child marriages contribute to virtually every social malaise that keeps India behind in women's rights. The problems include soaring birth rates, grinding poverty and malnutrition, high illiteracy and infant mortality and low life expectancy, especially among rural women.

Dowry

Women are kept subordinate, and are even murdered by the practice of dowry. A December 1997 article in *India Today,* entitled, *Victims of Sudden Affluence* states, "A woman on fire has made dowry deaths the most vicious of social crimes; it is an evil endemic to the subcontinent but despite every attempt at justice the numbers have continued to climb. With get-rich-quick becoming the new *mantra*, dowry became the perfect instrument for upward material mobility". A study done by a policy think-tank, the Institute of Development and Communication states, "the quantum of dowry exchange may still be greater among the upper classes, but 80 per cent of dowry deaths and 80 per cent of dowry harassment occurs in the middle and lower stratas".

The article goes on to state, "So complete is the discrimination among women that the gender bias is extended even.toward the guilty. In a bizarre trend, the onus of murder is often put on the women to protect the men. Sometimes it is by consent. Often, old mothers-in-law embrace all the blame to bail out their sons and husbands." Despite every stigma, dowry continues to be the signature of marriage. Says Renuka Dagar, "It is taken as a normative custom and dowry harassment as a part of family life".

Divorce

Divorce is not a viable option. Divorce is rare it is a considered a shameful admission of a woman's failure as a wife and daughter-in-law. In 1990, divorced women made up a miniscule

0.08 per cent of the total female population. Maintenance rights of women in the case of divorce are weak. Although both Hindu and Muslim law recognize the rights of women and children to maintenance, in practice, maintenance is rarely set at a sufficient amount and is frequently violated.

Both Hindu and Muslim personal laws fail to recognize matrimonial property. Upon divorce, women have no rights to their home or to other property accumulated during marriage; in effect, their contributions to the maintenance of the family and accumulation of family assets go unrecognized and unrewarded.

Inheritance

Women's rights to inheritance are limited and frequently violated. In the mid-1950s the Hindu Personal Laws, which apply to all Hindus, Buddhists, Sikhs and Jains, were overhauled, banning polygamy and giving women rights to inheritance, adoption and divorce. The Muslim Personal Laws differ considerably from that of the Hindus, and permit polygamy. Despite various laws protecting women's rights, traditional patriarchal attitudes still prevail and are strengthened and perpetuated in the home.

Under Hindu law, sons have an independent share in the ancestral property. However, daughters' shares are based on the share received by their father. Hence, a father can effectively disinherit a daughter by renouncing his share of the ancestral property, but the son will continue to have a share in his own right. Additionally, married daughters, even those facing marital harassment, have no residential rights in the ancestral home.

Even the weak laws protecting women have not been adequately enforced. As a result, in practice, women continue to have little access to land and property, a major source of income and long-term economic security. Under the pretext of preventing fragmentation of agricultural holdings, several States have successfully excluded widows and daughters from inheriting agricultural land.

Women in Public Office (Revised May 1999)

Panchayati Raj Institutions

The highest national priority must be the unleashing of woman-power in governance. That is the single most important source of societal energy that we have kept corked for half a century. Through the experience of the Indian Panchayati Raj Institutions (PRI) 1 million women have actively entered political life in India. The 73rd and 74th Constitutional Amendment Acts, which guarantee that all local elected bodies reserve one-third of their seats for women, have spearheaded an unprecedented social experiment which is playing itself out in more than 500,000 villages that are homes to more than 600 million people.

Institutionalization of Crime

The dowry system (payments from the bride's family to the groom or groom's family at the time of marriage) has a long history in India and many other Asian societies. The modern Indian dowry system has its roots in the traditional upper caste practices of *kanyadan* (literal meaning: gift of the virgin bride); *vardakshina* (voluntary gifts given by the bride's father to the groom); and *stridhan* (voluntary gifts given by relatives and friends to the bride). In the past, the dowry may have served as a form of presorted inheritance for women, because only men were entitled to inherit family property. It may also have been a form of compensation to the groom and his family for the economic support they would provide to the new wife, because women had little or no role in the productive economy and would be dependent upon their husbands and in-laws. However, the latter interpretation appears implausible, given that, in pre-British India, the bride price was prevalent among the upper castes (i.e., Brahmins) in southern India, even though women in these castes did not work outside their homes for status reasons.

This practice was later abandoned by the upper castes because it was equated with the "sale" of a girl; instead, the bride's family gave gifts voluntarily to the groom. If economic dependence of women is causally related to dowry practice, logically one should see a decrease in the incidence of the dowry with women's increasing role in the productive economy of this situation has a variety of consequences. Because daughters require extreme financial investments with no material return, rates of foemale foeticide and infanticide are high in some parts of the country. And the frequency and severity of violence against wives who bring too small a dowry to their marriages, perpetrated both by their husbands and their husbands' families, is a growing problem. Given that the historical functions of the dowry have largely disappeared, why are the practice becoming more widespread and the value of dowries inflating? The answer may be in part demographic. The mate selection system of India has long been characterized by hypergamy, with women from lower status families marrying higher status men within the same caste. This constrains the number of potential husbands available to women above the lowest status levels, particularly when combined with other selection restrictions such as village exogamy.

In recent years, High status families have been leading the way to lower fertility. This means there are fewer higher status men for women to marry, creating a "marriage squeeze" for women and intensifying the competition for suitable grooms. Because marriages are traditionally status-hypogenous, the dowry is also a vehicle by means of which brides' families make status claims. The size of the dowry provides the bride-giver with an opportunity for social advancement by attracting a groom from a higher position in the status hierarchy; the groom's family may select the economically most desirable bride from among a pool of eligible brides. Because the dowry is symbolic of the social and economic standing of the bride-giving family, ostentatious dowry payments increase the status of the bride's family. In addition, a bride's parents are likely to believe that a generous dowry is essential to ensure that their daughter is treated well in her new home. The parents-in-law may show preferential treatment to a daughter-in-law who brings a large dowry by giving her fewer household responsibilities, allowing more autonomy, and treating her more courteously.

Given the prevalence of dowry related violence, these concerns appear to be well founded. Young men and their families have come to see the dowry as a route to sudden affluence and rapid upward mobility. This route may be particularly attractive to men from the lower middle and lower social classes, where the means to upward social mobility are limited, inducing men in these classes to coerce their wives into bringing larger dowries in pursuit of their material aspirations. Further, the flow of resources from parents to daughters continues over the lifetime of the parents, in the form of monetary and material gifts to daughters' husbands and in-laws for every major occasion. When they arrange the marriage of a son, parents do not just look forward to the dowry they will receive at the wedding. They look at the bride's family's general capacity to give. In some cases, where these expectations are not fulfilled, wives may suffer severe consequences, including death. With all the real and potential adverse consequences of the dowry system for women, it is surprising in many ways that the custom is flourishing. But while women are regularly victims of dowry violence if their dowries are judged to be too small, they are also beneficiaries of the dowry system in some ways.

Women play major roles in negotiating dowries for their sons, in determining how the dowries will be used, and in harassing daughters-in-law for greater dowries and more gifts from their families. Thus, there are some reasons why women may be supportive of the dowry system. To understand why the dowry continues to be an influential part of the Indian mate selection system in spite of its problematic consequences, it is necessary to understand the attitudes of women toward it. On the other hand, modernizing influences are likely to reduce support for the dowry system. Younger women and those with more education are more likely to be exposed to modern ideas, and less likely to follow conventional customs, especially those that undermine the status of women such as the dowry. Women who are regularly exposed to the media are also likely to be less supportive of tradition.

Those who live in urban areas have more access to modern educational systems and media, and also are exposed to more cosmopolitan environments that challenge conventional thinking and lifestyles. Employed women are more likely to be exposed to liberal thinking and lifestyles in the workplace and their greater financial resources allow them to question traditional practices that pose burdens to their families and undermine their status. In terms of self-interest, the more unmarried sons a woman has the more she and her family are likely to benefit from the dowry system. Women with more daughters, conversely, will experience a greater financial burden because of the dowry system and are thus less likely to support it. In addition, women who are married consanguineously (that is, to husbands to whom they were related prior to marriage) are likely to have had a less aversive experience with the dowry. Dowries in such cases are usually smaller, because the groom's parents are hesitant to make exorbitant demands on relatives, and the bride's parents are often able to exercise some control over the disposition of the dowry. This means that the dowry is often used for the benefit of the newly married couple rather than the groom's parents.

Article 16 of the UN Convention on the Elimination of All Forms of Discrimination against Women (CEDAW) protects women's right to decide on the number and spacing of their children.

Understanding Social Reality

Human behaviour is influenced and shaped by social forces and personal characteristics. Work behaviour is social behaviour. To understand gender related issues one has to build a joint construct of individual agents and their social cultural context. This is even truer when the countries involved are oceans apart as in this study, i.e., the USA and India. Different nations have different cultural heritages which are values collectively held by a majority of population (possibly differentiated by social classes), and these values are transferred from generation to generation through education, early childhood experiences in the family, schools and through socialization in organizations and institutions. These values become social norms for that society. It is hard to see this process in one's own culture. A deep and painfully acquired empathy for other cultures is required before one becomes sensitive to the range of social norms, for truths in one society may be falsehoods in another.

Social learning theory emphasizes environmental factors as opposed to individual factors in the development of personality.

Achievement is a function of more or less ephemeral social expectations that are embodied in what we call norms. In a very real sense, a social group tells a person what to strive for as well as how to attain this end. The effect of such norms is clearly an important variable in an achievement situation.

Family and friends have a significant effect on occupational choices. Peer and parental expectations influence the vocational aspirations of youth. Girls have been taught not to aspire for high prestigious occupations. Sex role socialization leads women to focus on marriage rather than career. From this early experience comes the notion that one survives by marrying and taking care of the man, who must earn the living. Girls learn to satisfy their pleasure needs and their contribution needs by direct service to others.

Social values are changing in the USA as well as in the rest of the world. Worsening economic conditions need for two incomes per family, rising divorce rates, and insecurity in marriage are prompting women to plan and prepare for a career. Younger women realize that they are more likely to satisfy their survival needs directly through their own earnings rather than indirectly through the income of their spouses. Medical and technological advances such as amniocentesis, artificial insemination, *in vitro* fertilization and surrogate motherhood, provide women a greater control over their lives and bodies. Added to this is the concept of smaller families and longer life expectancy. These concepts give women more freedom and choice to plan and prepare for such eventualities.

Personality-Changing economic conditions may have driven women into the labour market, but after being in the workforce for a few decades they realize that paid employment along with satisfying their basic financial needs, also fulfils their individual needs of independence, provides them with a greater control of environment, and enables them to contribute more meaningfully to the societal and personal needs. Through the career they engage in productive work, develop skills and talents and find self-fulfilment the challenge of work that is valued by the society, gives them a sense of achievement, and a realization of self-worth. This gain of self-esteem in large part is instrumental in satisfying their pleasure and contributory needs. Recent studies of females in professional employment show that men and women do not differ in self-ratings, self-confidence and work values. Also, with the development of better measuring instruments of job evaluation there is a narrowing of the differences in the styles of management, motivation and leadership between males and females. Although most gender related issues like pay equity, sexual harassment, child care needs, flexible schedules, minority and healthcare issues, started as feminist agenda, yet both men and women have benefited from the debate, and the resultant solutions at the workplace. Thus one can conclude that the basic work motivation is the same for men and women, but due to early social and cultural influences we make different choices.

India presents a very interesting study of how class system of the West is no more egalitarian than the caste system of the East. At the beginning of this century Indian women did begin to move into professions like medicine and teaching. This happened as a response to the demand for education and healthcare among the female relatives of middle class men, and also because of sexual segregation. Female seclusion demanded that these services should be provided by other women. Government service and administrative jobs were opened to women after independence. At independence (1947) the Indian women's movement also succeeded in bringing women's legal position on a level with many rich countries of the West. Indian Constitution conferred equal rights and status to all citizens forbidding any discrimination on the grounds of caste, creed, religion or sex. Educated elite women who had played an active role during the independence movement took up leadership positions. By 1988 ten per cent of members of Parliament were women and eighteen per cent of women won in the State assembly elections compared to seventeen per cent of the men.

Increasing Number of Indian Women are preparing to take up Professional Careers

A majority of women in India as in the United States, however, are in feminist professions. Both societies place low status on such women's professions and pay them less than men. The Indian professional women also experience job segregation, as well as discrimination in selection, promotion, training and assessment. In employment restrictions are imposed on their physical mobility and their social interaction with males, by sexual harassment at work, and by gossip affecting all aspects of their lives. The employment may not release women from subordination, but it does provide the psychological basis for women to exert and exercise power. Educational attainment and employment does bring status to individual women. It improves their chances of marrying in a higher caste or status family. It also gives them economic independence.

In the family women's lives are controlled through male authority figure, by imposing the entire burden of domestic work upon them in addition to the paid work outside the home. Most men believe that domestic work and child care are not their job, and some of them consider it beneath their dignity to perform those tasks. Margaret Alva, a Member of Parliament combines many roles but is proud to be a wife and devoting-mother, a good part of her time is given to domestic duties.

Many successful women both in the USA and India are uncomfortable in discussing their professional achievements in front of their children and husbands, either because they are not relevant or disturbing to members of their family to whom they are a mother or wife. In many cases the husband is complimented for the achievements of the wife, and for his generosity to allow the wife to participate and contribute. By defining women as primary domestic workers and sexual and reproductive property of men, and by assigning priority to man's paid employment, the society devalues educational attainment, and economic and social contributions of women.

One of the major locations of women's subordination rests on the personal relations of the family. Personal arena is the place where women have to negotiate the conditions of their lives on individual bases. Men resist conceding their privilege. They do not want to forgo their domination of women. During the debates on the Hindu Code Bill, Pandit Nehru remarked :

> "When it came to implementing the principle of sexual equality in the domestic arena many nationalist men were forced to admit that whilst they were determined to resist national subordination they did not want to forgo their domination of women."

Employment may not release women from subordination, but it does provide them the psychological basis to exert and exercise power. Economic independence, self-confidence and personal achievement motivation are the only tools that serve the women well in negotiating their status in the family with their husbands and other family members. Women's employment marks a significant rejection of male control. The positive things about Indian culture for women are the great women of the past, Goddesses that have great powers, and that women too possess great power and virtue (*shakti*). The idea of women's power persists even today.

Indian women, who have travelled to western countries for education and have later sought employment, often find that ideas of gender and race inferiority augment the discrimination they encounter in those supposedly enlightened countries. The context of western domination imports not only the idea of women's inferiority in relation to men, but also a notion of Indian women's inferiority in relation to western women. The myth of the third world's inferiority helps justify continued western exploitation of India and its resources, which worsens the economic conditions in India. This in turn deteriorates the position of women's chances of education and employment and reinforces the notion that women are less capable than men. Multinational companies use this to limit the opportunities for women in employment. Basu, Amrita (ed.) (1995).

Sex

Sex showed significant difference on Perseverance; Social Acceptance; Reaction to Success/Failure; Fear of Success; and on Women as Manager Scale.

Perseverance

A two-way factorial analysis of variance by sex and country with the scale as a dependent variable showed a significant difference by country and sex. Average agreement among Indians was greater than the Americans. Average agreement among males was greater than average agreement among females.

Women as Managers Scale

Average agreement among Indians was greater than the Americans. On the average difference between females in both the countries was smaller than males. A high percentage of Indian males (39.7%) compared to the U.S.A males (1.5%) felt women should not hold responsible positions. Also, whereas only 3 per cent of the American male LIS students felt that women are not ambitious enough to be successful in managerial positions, 37 per cent of the Indian male students believed this to be the case. On the average difference between females in both the countries was smaller than for males. Governmental and Non-Governmental Organizations (NGOs) have initiated various programmes as a part of the strategy to implement policies. These programmes initiatives have also received support from regional and international organizations and agencies. Most of the NGO programmes are supported by funding as well as by technical assistance. Interaction between Variables Competitiveness and Women as Managers Scale showed a significant interaction by country.

Competitiveness

On the average agreement among Indians was greater than the Americans. In this study the statement, "I would rather work in a library that pays well" showed a significant relationship among the male and female respondents in the USA study, but not in the India study (USA study 79% females and 91% males *Vs* India study 64% females and 59% males agreed with the statement). More males in the USA and more females in India wanted to work for libraries that paid well. A greater percentage of Indian students liked competing against the clock than the American students.

In the business world women are perceived as being dependent, passive, and subjective, and as lacking in competitiveness, ambition and leadership abilities. They are perceived as emotional and unfit for managerial positions. The public due to stereotypical perceptions generally does not look upon women as leaders. In this study Indian males felt that women's emotions will not let them handle responsible positions more than the Americans cohorts.

RCH Services Programmes

The RCH Programme was launched nationwide in 1996 to provide holistic reproductive and child healthcare through the existing, vast network of the primary healthcare system. The RCH Programme encompasses provisions for all aspects of safe motherhood and child survival interventions, including a focus on increased access to contraceptives, safe management of unwanted pregnancies, enhanced nutrition, prevention and management of RTIs and STIs, availability of reproductive health services to adolescents, and educational outreach. The RCH Programme also focuses on providing services for gynaecological problem management and cancer screening for women. The programme has been in operation since 1996 and is being monitored through periodic nationwide, district based Rapid Household Surveys.

Integrated Child Development Services (ICDS) Scheme

The ICDS scheme offers an integrated package of early childhood care services. These services include supplementary feeding, immunization, health checkups, referral services for children up to six years of age and for expectant and nursing mothers, and nutrition and health education for mothers. The ICDS Scheme covers almost 85 per cent of the blocks in the country. There is an increasing focus on girl children under the scheme.

Adolescent Girl Scheme

This special intervention for girls aged 11–18 started in 1991–92 to meet their special nutrition, education, and skill development needs. This scheme has been extended to 3.9 million adolescent girls in 507 blocks throughout the country, which were selected through the ICDS scheme. The scheme also envisages imparting skills and encouraging the involvement of girls in useful economic activities later in life. The scheme has two subsets of target groups: the Girl-to-Girl Approach for adolescent girls aged 11–15 and *Balika Mandal*, which focuses on reaching adolescent girls aged 11–18. Under the scheme, an additional 1,493 blocks will be added to expand programme coverage.

State Plans of Action for the Girl Child

State governments are to formulate State Plans of Action for the Girl Child appropriate to the conditions prevailing in their respective States. Thus far, the governments of Karnataka, Madhya Pradesh, Tamil Nadu, and Goa have formulated State plans of action.

District Primary Education Programme

This Department of Education programme provides a special thrust to achieve universal coverage of primary education through decentralized planning and management, decentralized target setting, community mobilization, and district-and population-specific planning. Specific strategies have been designed to enhance girls' access, enrolment, and retention in the school system. At present, 219 districts in 15 States are covered under the programme. As a result, there has been a spurt in enrolment and an increase in learning achievements among girls. Increased community involvement, improvement in classroom processes, and a concerted equity focus have emerged as key success markers of the programme.

Balika Samridhi Yojana, 1997

This scheme works to raise the status of girl children born in families below the poverty line by providing financial help to these families. Some specific criteria have been laid down to provide financial assistance to the mother of a newborn girl child in the form of grants and investments through a postal financial instrument to be applied toward the education and economic independence of that child. The scheme also provides a scholarship provision for the girl's school education. The deposit will mature and be paid to the girl if she remains unmarried until she reaches 18 years of age. More than two million girls have benefited from the scheme so far.

National Plan of Action for the SAARC Decade of the Girl Child (1991–2000)

The heads of the government of the SAARC region declared 1991–2000 as the "SAARC Decade for Girl Child" and developed this plan of action. In fulfilment of this commitment, the Government of India identified "Survival, Protection, and Development" as a major theme, focusing on gender specific needs and requirements to the fullest possible extent. This was a conscious effort to ensure equitable rights, opportunities, benefits, and status to girl children. Several other initiatives that have been taken to promote the development of children and adolescents include the following :

- The Department of Education has been running a programme of non-formal education since 1979 to reach marginalized children in the 6–14 years old age group. The plan is being implemented in 25 States/ Urban Territories (UTs), particularly for those who have dropped out of school, working children, children in environments without schools, and girls who cannot attend formal-schools on account of domestic chores.
- The National Service Scheme (NSS) was launched in 1969 with a primary focus on students' personality development and community service. NSS involved more than 1.6 million student volunteers from more than 175 universities and 22 senior secondary councils. The scheme's programmes include "regular activities" and "special campaign programmes."
- *Bharat* Scouts and Guides, the third largest youth organization in the world, has enrolled 2.3 million guides and scouts. Scouting and guiding movements aim to develop boys' and girls' characters with the goal of making them good citizens of India. It inculcates

in them a spirit of patriotism and promotes balanced physical and mental development.

- The Ministry of Labour is running 76 national child labour projects in the country, covering 150,000 out-of-work children in 10 States/UTs with high unemployment levels. To ensure the welfare of these children, special schools have been set up to provide basic services such as non formal education, vocational training, supplementary nutrition, and health care.
- The Ministry of Social Justice and Empowerment has been implementing the "Integrated Programme for Street Children" since 1992–93. One of the important initiatives under the programme's revision in 1998 was the establishment of the Child Help Line Services in a number of cities. The Child Help Line provides emergency assistance to children. Continued involvement in the programme is based on the need of the child, who is referred to an appropriate organization for long-term follow-up and care. NGOs have addressed a range of issues related to the health and development of adolescents. These include reproductive and sexual health, general health, education, employment/skill development, gender equality, personality development, groups with special needs, and alcohol and drug abuse. Most of the NGOs work on sexuality is based on two distinct models: programmes focusing on providing information on sexual issues to unmarried adolescents, and programmes providing information and services.

Population Council

The Population Council has supported initiatives on adolescent transition in different States in collaboration with several NGOs, namely RUWSEC in Tamil Nadu, SUTRA in Himachal Pradesh, ADITHI in Bihar, CINI in West Bengal, and CHETNA in Gujarat and Rajasthan. The Population Council supported programmes on adolescence run by Mahila Samakhya in Karnataka and Andhra Pradesh and in the State of Haryana, *Apni Beti Apna Dhan* [Billing, M.S. (1991)].

MAMTA

The Health Institute for Mother and Child in New Delhi has made significant efforts to promote the cause of adolescent health.

Society for Social Uplift Through Rural Action (SUTRA)

Sutra is based in the hilly region of Jagjit Nagar, Himachal Pradesh and regularly undertakes training programmes, seminars/workshops, and courses for capacity building among various groups. These groups include *Mahila Mandals* (women's groups), *panchayats* (local governing councils), and *Yuvaki Sangathans* (adolescent girls' groups). The organization operates in five districts (Solan, Sirmaur, Mandi, Hamirpur, and Kullu) and 10 development blocks of Himachal Pradesh. The staff works closely with 400 Mahila mandals, 131 Yuvaki Sangathans, and 100 Gram Panchayats directly through training and convening meetings or through sister organizations. The activities are geared toward wide understanding of reproductive health. The encompassing issues are body care, menstruation, RTIs, abortion, family planning, sexual relations, violence, liquor, and adolescent health.

ADITHI

This non-governmental development organization, established

in Bihar in 1988, has been working on adolescent issues since 1995, focusing specifically on adolescent girls aged 11–18 years. ADITHI started Balika Kishori Chetna Kendras (awareness centres for young unmarried girls) with support from UNICEF. The aim of the Kendras is to build a community where women and men have equal status and importance. There are more than 18 Kendras in 18 villages, with a total of 465 participants, of which 351 participated regularly. These Kendras are now run with the support from Action Aid. There are about 20–25 girls in each centre. Unlike the non formal education centres, which are targeted at girls who have either never attended or dropped out of school, these centres are open to all, including girls attending schools or non-formal education centres.

Prerana

Prerana initiated adolescent programmes in 1987 and in 1990, Prerana further enhanced its initiatives by launching the Better Life Demonstration Project for girls and young women and a parallel programme of Better Life Development Programme for boys and young men. The objective of each programme is to create an environment of dignity and opportunity for adolescents, enabling them to achieve their full potential in terms of personal growth and ability to contribute to family, community, and societal development. The programmes were implemented as a development project in six villages along the periphery of Delhi. The programme targeted individuals and their peer groups, families, and communities. Learning modules included information, education, and services in the areas of personality development, education, health, reproductive health, economic participation, and life skills training. Over 5,000 adolescent girls and 1,800 adolescent boys have reached through direct field programmes.

CHETNA

This Ahemedabad based organization has been working on adolescent health issues in the State of Rajasthan and Gujarat. It works directly and indirectly with adolescent girls in an effort to build local capacity to address their needs. The organization conducts health camps in collaboration with local organizations and provides health services to adolescent girls. It also trains local organizations in the two States to raise awareness and address the needs of adolescent girls in their project area. Advocacy is also a key aspect of their programme.

India INCLEN

India INCLEN, in Lucknow, developed an instrument for reproductive health counselling in the hopes of educating sexually active adolescent boys about STIs and reducing their risk behaviour.

Healthy Adolescent Project in India (HAPI) Project

This project is based in West Bengal and works with guides and scouts in both the main city of Calcutta and other, less urban areas in the State. The project was initiated in 1999 with the support from the David and Lucile Packard Foundation.

Adolescent Girls' Health Project – Jabalpur

This ongoing, six-year programme was initiated with the support from CARE and is designed to address the reproductive health needs of nearly 32,000 adolescent girls, both married and unmarried, living in the slums of Jabalpur in Madhya Pradesh. CARE trains medical staff, community health workers, and traditional birth attendants in adolescent health issues, reproductive health care, and birth spacing.

Health care workers train adolescent girls to educate their peers through school and community group meetings. The focus is on establishing a network of Adolescent Girls' Health Guides. In addition, the project targets adolescent boys, husbands of adolescent girls, parents, teachers, and community leaders.

Pathfinder/India

Pathfinder's adolescent health programme will work in partnership with Indian NGOs, initially focusing on the provision of reproductive health information, education, counselling, and services for adolescents.

International Centre for Research on Women (ICRW)

ICRW is coordinating a multi-site intervention and research programme to develop effective programmes for adolescent sexual and reproductive health and development in India. The research has provided urban and rural community-based data on adolescents' lives, particularly their reproductive health needs. The studies confirmed that a lack of power, decision-making opportunity, autonomy, and access to resources underlie the reproductive health risks faced by adolescents, particularly adolescent females, and those who are unmarried. The project is being implemented in two phases. Phase I (1996–1999) addressed the paucity of basic research on adolescents in India and provided urban and rural community based data on adolescents' lives, particularly their reproductive needs. In Phase II (1999–2005), ICRW is collaborating with five organizations in India to test multiple intervention approaches addressing the adolescents' needs identified in Phase I.

Centre for Development and Population Activities (CEDPA)

CEDPA, an international NGO with operations in Delhi, in collaboration with local NGOs, UNFPA, UNESCO and USAID, has adapted "Choose a Future: Issues and Options for Adolescent Boys" to the Indian cultural context and is currently implementing programmes in 11 States. The package has been designed to effectively challenge gender inequalities and address male involvement. It helps to foster true partnerships in relationships, responsible fatherhood, and alternatives to violence.

Planned Parenthood Federation

Planned Parenthood has promoted four major projects with the help of local NGOs :

1. *Improving the Reproductive Health of Young Women and Men* : The goal of the project is to improve the lives of adolescents and youth by providing contraceptive services and sexuality education in 20 rural villages in a district in West Bengal with a local NGO.
2. *Couple to Couple : Improving the Reproductive Health of Young Couples in Rural India :* The project employs peer couples to work with groups of newly weds and other young couples to motivate them to increase gender awareness, encourage supportive relationships, and plan for their new families together. The aim of this project is to create an enabling environment for young couples to overcome social, cultural, and gender barriers to plan and space their children's births and achieve positive reproductive and child health.
3. *Improving the Reproductive Health of Adolescents*

and Youth : Located in Jharkhand State, the project aims to increase young people's knowledge and understanding about sexuality and reproductive health and help them develop communication and decision-making skills so that they may lead healthy reproductive lives.

4. *Reproductive Health through Advocacy and Services* : The project is a part of a larger programe to improve the reproductive health and rights of adolescents and youth in the Indian States of Bihar and West Bengal. The programme aims to improve the general reproductive health of adolescents and young people and develop the capacity of NGOs, private providers, and government facilities to plan, sustain, and advocate for adolescent and youth reproductive health programmes.

References

Amin, Sonli K. "Why Do Girls Drop Out?" *Social Welfare,* April, 2001.

Ashna, Pratima. *Women's Movement in India*. Delhi, Vikas. p.23, 1974.

Bacchi, Carol Lee. *Women, Policy and Politics: The Construction of Policy Problems*. Thousand Oaks, Calif.: Sage 1999.

Basu, Amrita (ed.). *The Challenge of Local Feminisms: Women's Movements in Global Perspective*. Boulder, Colo.: West View 1995.

Billing, M. S. "The marriage squeeze on high-caste Rajasthani women." *Journal of South Asian Studies,* 50 (2), 1991.

Bhat, P.N.M., and S.S. Halli."Demography of bride price and dowry: Causes and Consequences of the Indian marriage squeeze", *Population Studies,* 53 (2): 1999.

Caldwell, J. C., P. H. Reddy. "The causes of marriage change in South India."and P. Caldwell, *Population Studies,* 37 (3): 1983.

Caplan, L. "Bridegroom price in urban India: Class, Caste, and 'Dowry evil' among Christians in Madras", *Man,* 19 (2): 1984.

Das Gupta, M. "Selective discrimination against female children in rural Punjab, India." *Population and Development Review,* 13 (1), 1994.

—, and "Intensified gender bias in India: A consequence of P. N. M. Bhat fertility decline", in M. Krishnaraj, R. M. Sudarshan, and A. Shariff (eds.), *Gender, Population and Development*. Delhi: Oxford University Press. 1998.

DeMaris, A. "A tutorial in logistic regression." *Journal of Marriage and the Family,* 57 (4): 1995.

Desai, Sonalde. *Gender Inequalities and Demographic Behaviour: India.* New York: The Population Council, Inc. 1994.

Diwan, P. *Dowry and Protection to Married Women*. New Delhi: Deep & Deep Publications, 1987.

D'Souza, Victor S. " Family status and female work participation", In Alfred DeSouza (ed.), *Women in Contemporary India and South Asia*. New Delhi, Manohar, p. 129,1980.

Government of India. 1993 National Nutrition Policy. Department of Women and Child Development, 2001.

Government of India, 2000. National Population Policy of India. Ministry of Health and Family Welfare, Government of India.

Government of India. *Towards Equality: Report of the Commission on the Status of Women in India*. New Delhi, Government of India.

International Institute for National Family Health Survey, "Bihar 1992-93". Bombay: Population Sciences (IIPS). IIPS, 1995.

International Institute of Population Sciences (IIPS) 1993 and 1998. *Rapid Household Survey (RCH-RHS) Phases I & II.* Mumbai: International Institute of Population Sciences.

IIPS. 2000. *National Family Health Survey (NFHS-2)*. Mumbai: International Institute of Population Sciences.

Jhutti, J. "Dowry among Sikhs in Britain", in W. Menski (ed.), *South Asia and the Dowry Problem*. London: Trentham Books Ltd., 1998.

Kaila, H.L. "Gender Differences in Behaviour." *Social Welfare* 48(3). 2001.

Katz, J. *Career Values for Men and Women*, Paper presented at HRMOB. Association for Human Resources Management and Organizational Behaviour, 1988.

Kumari, R. *Brides Are Not for Burning: Dowry Victims in India*. New York : Advent Books, 1989.

McCoid, C. H. "Dowry Deaths in India: A materialist analysis." Working paper No. 188, Michigan State University. Minturn, L., 1989.

Ministry of Human Resource Development, Government of India

Nanda, B.R. (ed). *Indian Women from Purdah to Modernity*. New Delhi, Vikas, 1976.

Nadagouda, S. G., "Influence of socio-economic factors on the employed K. Saroj, and R. Aruna Hindu woman's attitude toward dowry." *Indian Journal of Social Work,* 53 (4), 1992.

National Crime Records, Crime *in India*. Ministry of Home Affairs, Government of *India*. 1998.

Omvedt, Gail. "Violence Against Women: New Movements and New Theories in India." *Kali Primaries*. 1990.

Paul, M. C. *Dowry and Position of Women in India: A Study of Delhi Metropolis*. New Delhi: Inter-India Publications. 1985.

Prasad, B. D. "Dowry-related violence: A content analysis of news in Selected newspapers." *Journal of Comparative Family Studies,* 25 (1): 1994.

Purushothaman, Sangeetha. *The Empowerment of Women in India: Grassroots Women's Networks and the State*. New Delhi: Sage Publications, 1998.

Rao, V. "Dowry influence in rural India: A statistical investigation." *Population Studies,* 47 (2): 1993.

Rao, V. "Dowry in North India: Its consequences for women", pp. 341-356 in Patricia Uberoi (ed.), *Family, Kinship and Marriage in India*. Delhi: Oxford University Press. 1993.

Registrar General, India, 1993. *Survey of Causes of Deaths*. Model Registration System. Registrar General, India.

Registrar General and Census Commissioner, 1991. *Census of India,* 1991. India: Registrar General and Census Commissioner.

Registrar General and Census Commissioner, 2001. *Census of India,* 2001. India: Registrar General and Census Commissioner.

Sarkar, Lotika and Mazumdar. "Note of Dissent," in Department of Social Welfare, *Towards Equality: Report of the Commission on the Status of Women in India*. New Delhi, Government of India, p.355, 1974.

Srinivas, M. N. *Some Reflections on Dowry*. Delhi: Oxford University Press, 1984.

Srinivasan, K., A. Shariff, India: *Towards Population and Development Goals*. United W. A. Zaman, and C. Bierring Nations Population Fund. Delhi: Oxford University Press, 1997.

Stone, L., and C. James *Dowry, bride-burning, and female power in India*. Women's Studies International Forum 18 (2): 125-134. Teja, M. K., 1995.

Stone, L., and C. James. *Dowry : A Study of Attitudes and Practices*. New Delhi: Inter-India Publications, 1991.

Subramaniam, Mangal. *Social Empowerment through Collective Process: The Local-Global Interface in the Case of Mahila Samakhya Karnataka (India)*. Ph.D. dissertation, Department of Sociology, University of Connecticut, 2000.

Susan, Gal. *Reproducing Gender: Politics, Publics and Everyday Life,* Gail Kligman, (ed.) *After Socialism*. Princeton N.J.: Princeton University Press, 2000.

Venkateswaran, Schindhya. *Environment, Development and the Gender Gap*. New Delhi: Sage Publications, 1995.

Appendix

AIDS	Acquired Immune Deficiency Syndrome
ARH	Adolescent Reproductive Health
ASFR	Age Specific Fertility Rate
CEDPA	Centre for Development and Population Activities
CSW	Commercial Sex Worker
DANIDA	Danish Agency for Development Assistance
FP	Family Planning
HAPI	Healthy Adolescent Project in India
HIV	Human Immune Deficiency Virus
ICDS	Integrated Child Development Services
ICMR	Indian Council of Medical Research
ICPD	International Conference on Population and Development
ICRW	International Centre for Research on Women
IEC	Information, Education, and Communication
IIHMR	Indian Institute of Health Management Research
IIPS	International Institute of Population Sciences
ILO	International Labour Organization
IUD	Intra Urterine Devices
MTP	Medical Termination of Pregnancy (Act)
NFHS	National Family Health Survey
NGO	Non-Governmental Organization

NSS	National Service Scheme
NSSO	National Sample Survey Organization
RCH	Reproductive and Child Health
RTI	Reproductive Tract Infection
RTI	Research Triangle Institute
RHS	Rapid Household Survey
SAARC	South Asian Association for Regional Cooperation
SERC	State Education Resource Centre
STI	Sexually Transmitted Infection
TFR	Total Fertility Rate
UN	United Nations
UNESCO	United Nations Educational, Scientific, and Cultural Organization
UNFPA	United Nations Population Fund
UNICEF	United Nations Children's Educational Fund
USAID	United States Agency for International Development
UT	Urban Territory or Union Territory
WHO	World Health Organization

3

Crime against Women

An Analysis of underlying Factors and Suggestions for Prevention

Harneet Chima

Crime against women is not a new phenomenon. Ever since we have documentation or written records, we come to know various crimes that have been committed against women. Crime and violence affect the lives of millions of women worldwide. In India, irrespective of socio-economic and educational classes it cuts across social, cultural and religious barriers. The problem of crime and violence against women has its roots in a socio-economic order that is heavily biased against women. An analysis of statistics on crime related to women reveal that the crime graph is climbing up higher and higher: (Table 3.1).

It is indeed ironical that in a country where women are put on a pedestal for worship, incidents of wife battering, rape, molestation, bride burning and other acts of crime against women keep on increasing. Women are subjected to crime and violence throughout their lives – not only since birth but also before birth.

Women find hardly any security at home; they are ill treated by husbands and in-laws and sexually assaulted even by their own father's brothers, and other male relations. They hardly have any security in the streets or outside homes, where they are subjected to vulgar comments, eve teasing, physical assault and even rape. Even in the workplace, they are often subjected

Table 3.1 : Gender Violence / Crime throughout Life Cycle.

Life Phase	*Type of violence / Crime*
Pre-birth	Selected sex abortion of the female foetus; wife battering during pregnancy to force an abortion.
Infancy	Female infanticide, death from malnutrition, starvation, neglect of girl child, rape.*
Childhood	Genital mutilation, child prostitution, child abuse and paedophilia, malnutrition, child marriage, rape.*
Adolescence	Sexual harassment, lewd comments and gestures, eve teasing, forced prostitution, trafficking of adolescent girls, abduction, sexual abuse at workplace (especially economic weaker girls), rape.*
Reproductive marital period	Dowry related physical and mental abuse, bride burning, dowry deaths, wife battering, marital rape, sexual harassment at workplace, home and outside, frequent pregnancies (against their wish) forced abortions, rape.*
Old age	Abuse of widows, economic deprivation, physical and mental abuse for money / property and even killing, rape.*

* *In the same year in Bhopal itself, a ninth month baby girl and a 65 years old woman was raped, which shows that female, of any age, is unsafe.*

to sexual harassment. The fear of crime and violence restricts their movements. Crime against women has increased to such an extent that women, for fear of crime and personal safety, are unable to contribute to the social and other affairs of the community.

If the data related to crime against women is analyzed, it shows that the National Crime Records Bureau's (1998) warning could come true that by 2010, the growth rate of crime against women would be higher than population growth rate. The International Centre for Research on Women (ICRW) report says that domestic violence kills more women each year than accidents or cancer.

The figures of reported criminal acts against women can be obtained from the records compiled by the Ministry of Home Affairs; the Police Research Bureau and the National Institute of Social Defence. But these facts and figures relate only to 'reported' cases of crime. The word "reported" deserves attention, because very few cases of crimes against women, be it rape, wife battering, mental torture or any other criminal acts are reported. This holds true not only for Madhya Pradesh, but for the whole of India. In the *Hindustan Times* (11th September, 2005) there was a front page news which said that "Gang admits to 40 unreported rape cases at Bhojpur, sex crimes saga continued for over 8 years. Recently, 8 men had also gang raped a woman". The paper reported that posing as cops, the 8 members gang would extort money, send away the men for more money and rape the women. They even filmed the acts and blackmailed the victims. Fearing social stigma, the victims remained silent. The Obaidullaganj police appealed to unknown victims to come out and lodge a formal complaint failing which, the culprits might not get the punishment they deserved." Acts of violence and crime against women continue to occur and reoccur despite constitutional provisions and legal protections. The reasons for crime against women require to be analysed, so that appropriate measures can be taken.

Social Causes and Crime against Women

Crime against women is directly related to the social structure, social customs, beliefs and practices. In a society where patriarchy is the order, women have a lower status, which is also the case in India and Madhya Pradesh. There has always been a strong link between patriarchy and prevalence of social inequalities, where the women have been relegated to a subordinate position. As inequality increases, crime and violence also increase. Discrimination and a lower position to women, accorded by society, results in the death of countless women. In India, if women gives birth only to daughters, she is verbally and physically abused by her husband and in-laws. Often, enable to bear the atrocities, women end up committing suicide. There are cases where parents kill their young daughter, as they are unable to fulfil the demands of dowry. Instances have also come to light, where daughters have committed suicide due to their father's inability to fulfil the demands of dowry.

In a patriarchal society, the dominance of men over women has to be maintained. Violence against women, like beating, rape, etc., is a maintenance mechanism of a patriarchal society, as well as a means of perpetuating the subordinate status of women and maintaining the dominance of men. The low social, economic and political position of women makes them easy and soft targets.

Customs and Beliefs

Many customs and practices in a society also are responsible for crime against women. One such custom, the custom of giving dowry has resulted in the death of many girls and women, as well as physical and mental torture. The custom of spending money on various ceremonies related to girls life—ear boring, expenses on marriage, expenses during the first year of marriage, expenses connected with pregnancy, etc., which the parents can ill-afford, often result in the ill-treatment of girls and even their death.

The custom of *sati* is not new to Indian society. Women have been burnt alive, willingly or unwillingly, along with their dead husbands. Even after passing of the Sati Prevention Act, we come across cases of Sati Roop Kanwar is an example. There are other such examples also. Crime against women is perpetuated in the name of customs and rituals. The *devadasi* system, the custom of dedicating low-caste *dalit* girls to a God or goddess, leads to their sexual exploitation and forces them into prostitution. Nepal's Devi System is similar. Burning of women as witches because they have been identified as the cause of a calamity by a local person or a sooth sayer, who is considered an expert on indigenous occult practices, has been recorded as a form of crime that occurs in West Bengal in India.

Also, there is a belief that sacrificing a girl before a goddess pleases the goddess, who bestows wealth and the bounties of life on the person who has done so. This belief has also resulted in the sacrifice of many innocent girls. Again, there is a belief that sex with a virgin girl will cure a man of illness and disease and bestow vitality. This again has resulted in the rape of many girls. Thus, it can be said that the genesis of discrimination, cruelty and crime against women can be traced to our social customs and practices rooted in culture and tradition. According to a World Health Organization report, due to customary practices, more than 80 million women have undergone female genital mutilation in Africa alone; 2 million women also risk this mutilation every year.

Family Relationships

One of the reasons for the rise in crime against women is the changing family structure and weakening of family ties. The disintegration of the joint family in India and Madhya Pradesh is one such reason. The joint family provided emotional, financial and physical support to all its members, whether young or old and exercised informal control over its members. It played an important role in teaching children basic values like truth, tolerance of others, respect for not only their mother and sisters, but also respect for other female members of the household. The joint family offered warmth and intimacy and a feeling of security. The members belonged; there was no sense of alienation. But now-a-days, the joint family is being replaced by the nuclear family. Often, in order to fulfil the economic demands, both husband and wife work. The domestic household is isolated. There is nobody at home to manage the children and instill proper values. The parents too are under constant strain, trying to cope up with the demands of the job and the children. Thrown back entirely on its own resources, the nuclear family becomes like an overloaded electrical circuit. When demands increase, fuses blow out. The victims are often women and girls, living in the family. Gelles (1979) has said that women are more likely to be hit, beaten up, injured or even killed by their own family members. Levinson (1989) went through the records cf human area files at Yale University and maintained that wife beating is the most common form of violence around the world. Aggression against women, incest, rape and other crimes often go unreported. The main reasons are that the victims often are financially dependent on their family members and are well aware of the fact that if they report the crime, they may be thrown out of the house and then be at the mercy of strangers, who might further exploit them. Fear of reprisals, even more abuse, also prevents a woman from reporting crimes committed by family members. Even when the women are economically independent, fear of society and embarrassment prevents them from reporting crimes committed by family members.

Urban Anomie

With urbanization increasing at a fast paçe, Urban Anomie is also increasing. In most urban towns, there is a heterogeneous population, consisting of people from various fields of life, religion, caste, economic strata, etc. Often, people from rural areas and other areas come to towns and settle there. Anonymity in urban areas makes it easier for males to commit crimes against women. Lack of family control, lack of worry about what neighbours and other people will think, if they are caught, encourage men to commit crimes against women. Fear of recognition and identification, which is a deterrent in familiar surroundings, is not there in cities. Also, many women in towns go out to work. Often, they are not escorted by anyone and as such make easy targets for men, who identify such women and plan their crimes. It is perhaps due to this urban anomie that places in Madhya Pradesh, like Bhopal, having a very high rate of crime; this also holds true about other towns.

Power Equations

The Indian society is male dominated. The woman is accorded a low status in life and is never an entity in her own right, she is always a daughter, a wife or a mother first and a woman later. Even in spite of changes in the society, the thinking of men about the submissive and dependent role of woman has not changed. On the other hand, due to education and awareness of their rights as well as increased economic independence, the women want to prove themselves and show that they are able to compete with men and stand on an equal footing, something that most men even now do not want. Men do not hesitate to use brute force and physical violence and sexual assault to keep women pinned down to prove their superiority. The analysis of crime and violence shows that the fear of violence, is one of the mechanisms through which domination is maintained and subordination ensured; resulting in an increase in the number of crimes. Men use violence as a form of social control. Crime against women in all its myriad forms, is the vengeance of masculine hubris against feminine ascendance in various domains of life threatening to destabilize man's supposed superiority.

It is a matter of common observation that in times of war, political upheaval and communal conflicts, it is the women who are raped, even though they are innocent and uninvolved. This is done to maintain the superiority of men, not just over women but also over other men of the opposite side, by humiliating their women. Power rapes, mass rapes are aimed at not just the women, but as a tool to humiliate and demoralize the group and community to which the victim belongs. Bart has said "rape is a power trip, not a passion trip".

Thus, we can say that crime and violence against women is the result of the perceived power relations that exist between men and women in society and to some extent the underlying tension dormant in any power sharing arrangement.

Police and Crime against Women

The role of the police in checking and preventing crime is very important as the police is the first agency and the first line of defence against crimes. But in India, the role of the police in checking crime has been dubious and lacking. Police inefficiency, corruption, police-politician nexus and connivance with the guilty is one of the cause of crimes against women. Women being raped in police custody is not something new. Women do not want to go and lodge a complaint in the police stations because they fear for their safety. Hardly any woman, educated or uneducated, would like to go to a police station as they find that the police personnel, especially at the lower ranks, have a unsympathetic attitude. They jeer, taunt, insult the women. Women are often afraid of policemen, which reflects the sad state of affairs in the country. The people (police personnel) in whom the victims, especially the women, should have utmost faith in, are the ones in whom the women have the least faith. The protection offered by the police to the men guilty of crimes against women, also discourages women to report against the culprits. A report in the *Hindustan Times* (September 16, 2005) says that a woman was raped by an M.L.A. The girl was rescued by the police on September 1, 2005 from the M.L.A's house in the evening, even though her father had lodged a complaint in the morning. The paper further reported that under the M.L.A's pressure, the personnel of Laor police station made her stay at the police station at night, where the station in-charge beat her up and made her change her statement. How can crime against women be prevented, when police personnel are hand-in-glove with the accused. The number of Mahila Police Thanas are also very less and needs to be increased.

Personality Traits of the Victim and the Victimizer

Most of the crimes against women are a result of marred mental outlook of men, depravity and a defective psychological state. For many criminals, crime against women is simply a way to dominate, to assert in a way that they are 'men'. Temperamental incompatibility in ways of thinking between husband and wife often results in the husbands beating the wife, to make her submissive. An analysis of men who commit crimes against women shows that these men often are ones who suffer from depression, low self-esteem and inferiority complex. They lack resources, skills and have a sociopathic personality and suffer from personality disorders. Often they are men who have been victims of violence in childhood, who are frequent users of alcohol, who face stressful situations, both at home or at work and who have tendency to try to dominate and who are possessive and suspicious by nature.

As far as women are concerned, we find that women who are submissive, feel helpless, depressed, have a poor, self-image or those who suffer from altruistic powerlessness are more likely the ones against whom crime are committed. In fact many rapists have said that they often look for "submissive' women.

Economic factors

Economic factors like poverty, unemployment (both of the

husband or the wife) create stressful situations and result in an increase in crime against women. Studies reveal that women who are unemployed and dependent on their husbands are more prone to violence than women who are in a position to fend for themselves. Women from lower economic strata are also more likely to be victims of crimes like rape, battering, prostitution, etc. It is not uncommon to read about atrocities on women of weaker economic sections, tribal women and *dalit* women. One thing common amongst them is that they all belong to the lower economic strata. Madhya Pradesh has the dubious distinction of having the highest crime rate against tribal women in India.

Another factor that has resulted in rising crimes against women is the unemployment of the husband, which has become a common phenomenon due to the growth of population, mechanization, pressure on land, etc. This creates a sense of frustration in the minds of the husband and beating a wife and subjecting her to 'marital rape' is a sort of vent for the feelings of frustration of the husband. Many times, a woman is left to fend for the family and fulfil its needs. This too results in feelings of inadequacy and inferiority in the minds of the husband's, they become over possessive and suspicious, thinking she is having a good time outside and that she is looking down upon the husband, since he is not earning. Acts of crime and violence against the woman are the result of an attempt by the husband to subdue his wife, assert his manliness and cut her down to size.

Laws

Although men and women have been granted the same rights and equality before law, a woman in India continues to be a victim of crime, exploitation and discrimination. In spite of numerous laws; some formed specifically to protect women, it is clear that these laws and notions of equality are confined more to books. The laws are full of loopholes and men and lawyers cleverly make use of these to prevent the women from getting justice. Not many women are in a position to engage lawyer. Men, due to their economic independence get to engage better lawyers. Often, the men try to delay the course of justice by asking for constant adjournments on the flimsiest of grounds. Tired of repeated trips to the court, unable to cope with the legal expenses, even the few women who manage to muster courage to go to court, ultimately give up in midway. Also, in cases of domestic violence and other crimes, there are very few people who are willing to stand up in court and testify in her favour. People consider it a private affair and do not want to get involved in legal matters. Further, statistics reveal that in few cases is the accused punished and often gets a less adequate punishment. All these legal procedures and hassles result in the ineffectiveness of laws in dealing with crime against women.

The Quick- Rich Factor

The materialistic culture and get rich quick factor is also responsible for increasing crimes against women. Prostitution is a quick way to earn money. Men often lure innocent girls and helpless women with promises of employment and help and lead them into prostitution. We also come across cases where girls themselves, some from middle class families, work as call girls to make money and fulfil their ever-growing needs. On 24th September, 2005, there was news on NDTV about girls belonging to respectable middle class families in Bhopal and Ujjain, who were working as call girls and were available on mobile phones. Such instances are not just confirmed to Madhya Pradesh but have been reported from different parts of India too.

Suggestions for Prevention of Crime against Women

The first and foremost step in prevention of crimes against women is identification of the various cause and factors which lead to various crimes against women and effective measures to check these. A holistic multi-pronged attack against crime is required. The government and laws alone cannot bring about a change in the condition of women. Change in the structure of the society is also needed, so that women are treated as equal members of the society. The reason why so many women put up with abuse and violence, both in the home and outside is primarily due to their unequal position in society and the fact that they have no other viable alternatives available to them. Also, reporting crimes like rape brings further 'shame' to the victim, for she is totally cut off from the society and even shunned by her own family members, as if she is responsible for the state of affairs. It is years of social conditioning, both of the men (who think they are born to dominate) and women (who are made to think they have an inferior position in society and must put up with all atrocities) which results in crime. Crime against women cannot be stopped until the exploitative structure of society itself is transformed.

Women seem to have accepted misery and exploitation as part of their fate and learnt to live with it. Centuries of male domination has destroyed their self-image and they feel they are not equal to men. Women need to be economically independent. They need to have a say in the decision-making processes, both at house and at the national level. But this is not so. The representation of women in legislatures and judicial bodies is very low.

There is need to create awareness among women about their rights. There is need to tell women to exercise these rights and not stay quiet. When crimes against them are committed, there is need to help them in exercising their rights by strengthening women's organizations and movements.

There is need also for a change in the criminal justice system. As far as the courts are considered, the judges should be gender–sensitized. The victims of crime should be rendered quick justice for as the saying goes 'Justice delayed is justice denied' and the accused must be given punishment and not allowed to walk away.

The press can play an important role in the crusade against crimes related to women. It should give adverse publicity to the perpetrators of crime and create public opinion against them, while at the same protecting the identity of the victim. The convictions awarded to the accused should also be given wide publicity, so that it serves as a deterrent to others.

The various measures which can be undertaken to prevent and lessen crimes against women are :

- Identification of the underlying factors leading to crimes.
- Increase in awareness level of women.
- Increase in economic empowerment and employment opportunities of women.
- Increased efforts to eliminate discrimination in terms and conditions of employment.
- Provision of support in the form of legal aid and quick disposal of cases.
- Moral and material support to women and establishment of shelter houses, where women along with children can be provided security.
- Promotion of supportive network at workplace.
- Gender sensitization of law enforcement agencies, policy-makers, administrators, etc.
- Free legal counselling.
- Formulation of new laws related to women and plugging the loopholes of the existing laws strict enforcement of existing laws and active support of government agencies, leaders, voluntary organizations and people in general.
- Media involvement to create awareness about equal status and rights of women and publicity against gender violence and crimes against women.

- Encouragement and enhancement of a greater participation of women in decision-making and policy making.
- Setting up of more Mahila Thanas and special 'crime against women cells' to deal with such crimes.
- Sensitizing the police personnel towards problems of women and encouraging them to deal with victims in a sympathetic manner.
- Encouraging women to come forward to report atrocities and crimes committed against them.
- Mobilization of the masses to support victims and encouraging the masses to condemn the accused not the victim.
- Recognition of the economic value of women's contribution to work in the house, agriculture, etc.
- Recognition of women's pivotal role in society, as well as in the home.
- Removal of gender bias in the minds of males and females. Starting from school and beginning in the home.
- Increasing the collection of documentation and research on gender violence and crime against women.
- Removal of practices rooted in our culture and tradition, which lead to atrocities and crime against women.

Table 3.2 : Incidence and Rate of Crime committed against Women In States, UTs and Cities during 2003

Sl. No.	*State/UT*	*Incidence*	*Percentage Contribution to All-India Total*	*Estimated Mid-Year Population (In lakhs)*	*Rate of Total Cognizable Crimes*	*Rank **	*Rank ***
(1)	**(2)**	**(3)**	**(4)**	**(5)**	**(6)**	**(7)**	**(8)**
STATES							
1.	ANDHRA PRADESH	18382	13.1	778.7	23.6	1	1

Table 3.2 (contd...)

(1)	(2)	(3)	(4)	(5)	(6)	(7)	(8)
2.	ARUNACHAL PRADESH	139	0.1	11.3	12.3	15	25
3.	ASSAM	5312	3.8	277.3	19.2	6	12
4.	BIHAR	5900	4.2	867.7	6.8	27	8
5.	CHHATTISGARH	3336	2.4	217.2	15.4	12	15
6.	GOA	121	0.1	14.3	8.5	25	28
7.	GUJARAT	5735	4.1	526.4	10.9	19	10
8.	HARYANA	4170	3.0	220.4	18.9	7	14
9.	HIMACHAL PRADESH	729	0.5	62.5	11.7	17	21
10.	JAMMU & KASHMIR	2164	1.5	107.3	20.2	4	19
11.	JHARKHAND	2488	1.8	280.0	8.9	24	17
12.	KARNATAKA	5834	4.1	543.7	10.7	20	9
13.	KERALA	5653	4.0	326.2	17.3	8	11
14.	MADHYA PRADESH	14547	10.3	633.7	23.0	2	2
15.	MAHARASHTRA	11273	8.0	1003.1	11.2	18	5
16.	MANIPUR	137	0.1	24.8	5.5	33	26
17.	MEGHALAYA	69	0.0	23.9	2.9	34	29
18.	MIZORAM	147	0.1	9.2	15.9	11	24
19.	NAGALAND	25	0.0	20.8	1.2	35	31
20.	ORISSA	4946	3.5	378.2	13.1	14	13
21.	PUNJAB	2375	1.7	251.1	9.5	23	18
22.	RAJASTHAN	11812	8.4	593.3	19.9	5	4
23.	SIKKIM	37	0.0	5.6	6.6	28	30
24.	TAMIL NADU	8888	6.3	635.9	14.0	13	6
25.	TRIPURA	537	0.4	32.9	16.3	10	22
26.	UTTAR PRADESH	12840	9.1	1743.8	7.4	26	3
27.	UTTRANCHAL	886	0.6	88.3	10.0	22	20
28.	WEST BENGAL	8508	6.1	828.3	10.3	21	7
TOTAL (STATES)		**136990**	**97.4**	**10505.9**	**13.0**	—	—
UNION TERRITORIES							
29	A & N ISLANDS	22	0.0	3.7	5.9	31	32
30	CHANDIGARH	159	0.1	9.6	16.6	9	23
31	D & N HAVELI	13	0.0	2.3	5.6	32	33
32	DAMAN & DIU	10	0.0	1.7	6.0	30	34
33	DELHI	3282	2.3	148.3	22.1	3	16
34	LAKSHADWEEP	4	0.0	0.6	6.3	29	35
35	PONDICHERRY	121	0.1	10.1	12.0	16	27
TOTAL (UTs)		**3611**	**2.6**	**176.35**	**20.5**	—	—
TOTAL (ALL-INDIA)		**140601**	**100.0**	**10682.1**	**13.2**		

* Rank on the basis of Rate of Total Cognizable Crimes (Column I6)

** Rank on the basis of Percentage Share (Column 4).

Source: NRCW — National Resource Centre for *Women.*

Table 3.3 : Incidence of Crimes Committed against Women during 2003

Sl. No.	State / UT	Estimated Mid-Year Population (In lakhs)	Rape			Kidnapping & Abduction			Dowry Deaths			Cruelty by Husband and Relatives		
			I	R	P	I	R	P	I	R	P	I	R	P
(1)	(2)	(3)	(4)	(5)	(6)	(7)	(8)	(9)	(10)	(11)	(12)	(13)	(14)	(15)
1.	ANDHRA PRADESH	778.73	946	1.2	6.0	931	1.2	7.0	466	0.6	7.5	8167	10.5	16.1
2.	ARUNACHAL PRADESH	11.30	31	2.7	0.2	51	4.5	0.4	0	0.0	0.0	14	1.2	0.0
3.	ASSAM	277.25	1095	3.9	6.9	1351	4.9	10.2	60	0.2	1.0	1808	6.5	3.6
4.	BIHAR	867.74	985	1.1	6.2	674	0.8	5.1	909	1.0	14.6	1880	2.2	3.7
5.	CHHATTISGARH	217.21	898	4.1	5.7	149	0.7	1.1	79	0.4	1.3	601	2.8	1.2
6.	GOA	14.25	31	2.2	0.2	13	0.9	0.1	2	0.1	0.0	24	1.7	0.0
7.	GUJARAT	526.39	236	0.4	1.5	859	1.6	6.5	54	0.1	0.9	3684	7.0	7.3
8.	HARYANA	220.40	353	1.6	2.2	271	1.2	2.0	222	1.0	3.6	1618	7.3	3.2
9.	HIMACHAL PRADESH	62.49	126	2.0	0.8	96	1.5	0.7	6	0.1	0.1	221	3.5	0.4
10.	JAMMU & KASHMIR	107.33	211	2.0	1.3	615	5.7	4.6	10	0.1	0.2	71	0.7	0.1
11.	JHARKHAND	280.03	712	2.5	4.5	262	0.9	2.0	262	0.9	4.2	559	2.0	1.1
12.	KARNATAKA	543.70	321	0.6	2.0	244	0.4	1.8	194	0.4	3.1	1704	3.1	3.4
13.	KERALA	326.20	394	1.2	2.5	102	0.3	0.8	33	0.1	0.5	2930	9.0	5.8
14.	MADHYA PRADESH	633.66	2738	4.3	17.3	608	1.0	4.6	648	1.0	10.4	2938	4.6	5.8
15.	MAHARASHTRA	1003.09	1268	1.3	8.0	626	0.6	4.7	368	0.4	5.9	5452	5.4	10.8
16.	MANIPUR	24.78	18	0.7	0.1	71	2.9	0.5	0	0.0	0.0	4	0.2	0.0
17.	MEGHALAYA	23.90	40	1.7	0.3	10	0.4	0.1	0	0.0	0.0	4	0.2	0.0
18.	MIZORAM	9.23	54	5.9	0.3	2	0.2	0.0	0	0.0	0.0	3	0.3	0.0
19.	NAGALAND	20.75	14	0.7	0.1	3	0.1	0.0	0	0.0	0.0	0	0.0	0.0
20.	ORISSA	378.21	725	1.9	4.6	373	1.0	2.8	279	0.7	4.5	1289	3.4	2.5
21.	PUNJAB	251.13	380	1.5	2.4	295	1.2	2.2	110	0.4	1.8	987	3.9	1.9
22.	RAJASTHAN	593.32	1050	1.8	6.6	1750	2.9	13.2	389	0.7	6.3	5733	9.7	11.3
23.	SIKKIM	5.61	10	1.8	0.1	0	0.0	0.0	0	0.0	0.0	1	0.2	0.0

(Contd...)

Table 3.3 : *(Contd...)*

(1)	(2)	(3)	(4)	(5)	(6)	(7)	(8)	(9)	(10)	(11)	(12)	(13)	(14)	(15)
24.	TAMIL NADU	635.87	557	0.9	3.5	632	1.0	4.8	220	0.3	3.5	1555	2.4	3.1
25.	TRIPURA	32.94	114	3.5	0.7	29	0.9	0.2	20	0.6	0.3	247	7.5	0.5
26.	UTTAR PRADESH	1743.80	911	0.5	5.7	1499	0.9	11.3	1322	0.8	21.3	2626	1.5	5.2
27.	UTTARANCHAL	88.25	107	1.2	0.7	134	1.5	1.0	93	1.1	1.5	317	3.6	0.6
28.	WEST BENGAL	828.33	1002	1.2	6.3	801	1.0	6.0	329	0.4	5.3	4948	6.0	9.8
TOTAL (STATES)		**10505.89**	**15327**	**1.5**	**96.7**	**12451**	**1.2**	**93.6**	**6075**	**0.6**	**97.9**	**49385**	**4.7**	**97.4**
UNION TERRITORIES														
29.	A & N ISLANDS	3.73	2	0.5	0.0	2	0.5	0.0	0	0.0	0.0	7	1.9	0.0
30.	CHANDIGARH	9.55	18	1.9	0.1	28	2.9	0.2	1	0.1	0.0	93	9.7	0.2
31.	D & N HAVELI	2.33	1	0.4	0.0	4	1.7	0.0	0	0.0	0.0	2	0.9	0.0
32.	DAMAN & DIU	1.68	5	3.0	0.0	1	0.6	0.0	1	0.6	0.0	0	0.0	0.0
33.	DELHI	148.28	490	3.3	3.1	797	5.4	6.0	130	0.9	2.1	1211	8.2	2.4
34.	LAKSHADWEEP	0.63	2	3.2	0.0	0	0.0	0.0	0	0.0	0.0	1	1.6	0.0
35.	PONDICHERRY	10.05	2	0.2	0.0	13	1.3	0.1	1	0.1	0.0	4	0.4	0.0
TOTAL (UTs)		**176.25**	**520**	**3.0**	**3.3**	**845**	**4.8**	**6.4**	**133**	**0.8**	**2.1**	**1318**	**7.5**	**2.6**
TOTAL (ALL-INDIA)		**10682.14**	**15847**	**1.5**	**100.0**	**13296**	**1.2**	**100.0**	**6208**	**0.6**	**100.0**	**50703**	**4.7**	**100.0**

Table 3.3 : (Contd...)

Sl. No.	State / UT	Molestation			Eve-Teasing (Sexual Harassment)			Importation of Girls			Sati Prevention Act		
		I	R	P	I	R	P	I	R	P	I	R	P
(1)	(2)	(16)	(17)	(18)	(19)	(20)	(21)	(22)	(23)	(24)	(25)	(26)	(27)
States													
1.	ANDHRA PRADESH	4128	5.3	12.5	2286	2.9	18.5	5	0.0	10.9	0	0.0	0.0
2.	ARUNACHAL PRADESH	43	3.8	0.1	0	0.0	0.0	0	0.0	0.0	0	0.0	0.0
3.	ASSAM	878	3.2	2.7	6	0.0	0.0	0	0.0	0.0	0	0.0	0.0
4.	BIHAR	688	0.8	2.1	11	0.0	0.1	37	0.0	80.4	0	0.0	0.0
5.	CHHATTISGARH	1481	6.8	4.5	105	0.5	0.9	0	0.0	0.0	0	0.0	0.0
6.	GOA	19	1.3	0.1	7	0.5	0.1	0	0.0	0.0	0	0.0	0.0
7.	GUJARAT	722	1.4	2.2	92	0.2	0.7	0	0.0	0.0	0	0.0	0.0
8.	HARYANA	344	1.6	1.0	1302	5.9	10.6	0	0.0	0.0	0	0.0	0.0
9.	HIMACHAL PRADESH	250	4.0	0.8	18	0.3	0.1	0	0.0	0.0	0	0.0	0.0
10.	JAMMU & KASHMIR	875	8.2	2.7	376	3.5	3.1	0	0.0	0.0	0	0.0	0.0
11.	JHARKHAND	424	1.5	1.3	2	0.0	0.0	0	0.0	0.0	0	0.0	0.0
12.	KARNATAKA	1585	2.9	4.8	84	0.2	0.7	0	0.0	0.0	0	0.0	0.0
13.	KERALA	1947	6.0	5.9	68	0.2	0.6	0	0.0	0.0	0	0.0	0.0
14.	MADHYA PRADESH	6848	10.8	20.8	705	1.1	5.7	0	0.0	0.0	0	0.0	0.0
15.	MAHARASHTRA	2661	2.7	8.1	682	0.7	5.5	0	0.0	0.0	0	0.0	0.0
16.	MANIPUR	44	1.8	0.1	0	0.0	0.0	0	0.0	0.0	0	0.0	0.0
17.	MEGHALAYA	13	0.5	0.0	1	0.0	0.0	0	0.0	0.0	0	0.0	0.0
18.	MIZORAM	88	9.5	0.3	0	0.0	0.0	0	0.0	0.0	0	0.0	0.0
19.	NAGALAND	4	0.2	0.0	2	0.1	0.0	0	0.0	0.0	0	0.0	0.0
20.	ORISSA	1669	4.4	5.1	188	0.5	1.5	1	0.0	2.2	0	0.0	0.0
21.	PUNJAB	346	1.4	1.1	199	0.8	1.6	0	0.0	0.0	0	0.0	0.0
22.	RAJASTHAN	2715	4.6	8.2	33	0.1	0.3	1	0.0	2.2	0	0.0	0.0
23.	SIKKIM	25	4.5	0.1	0	0.0	0.0	0	0.0	0.0	0	0.0	0.0

(Contd...)

(1)	(2)	(16)	(17)	(18)	(19)	(20)	(21)	(22)	(23)	(24)	(25)	(26)	(27)
24.	TAMIL NADU	2022	3.2	6.1	881	1.4	7.1	1	0.0	2.2	0	0.0	0.0
25.	TRIPURA	127	3.9	0.4	0	0.0	0.0	0	0.0	0.0	0	0.0	0.0
26.	UTTAR PRADESH	1098	0.6	3.3	4970	2.9	40.3	0	0.0	0.0	0	0.0	0.0
27.	UTTARANCHAL	136	1.5	0.4	98	1.1	0.8	0	0.0	0.0	0	0.0	0.0
28.	WEST BENGAL	1186	1.4	3.6	71	0.1	0.6	1	0.0	2.2	0	0.0	0.0
TOTAL (STATES)		**32366**	**3.1**	**98.3**	**12187**	**1.2**	**98.9**	**46**	**0.0**	**100.0**	**0**	**0.0**	**0.00**
UNION TERRITORIES													
29.	A & N ISLANDS	9	2.4	0.0	2	0.5	0.0	0	0.0	0.0	0	0.0	0.0
30.	CHANDIGARH	11	1.2	0.0	4	0.4	0.0	0	0.0	0.0	0	0.0	0.0
31.	D & N HAVELI	4	1.7	0.0	0	0.0	0.0	0	0.0	0.0	0	0.0	0.0
32.	DAMAN & DIU	3	1.8	0.0	0	0.0	0.0	0	0.0	0.0	0	0.0	0.0
33.	DELHI	489	3.3	1.5	105	0.7	0.9	0	0.0	0.0	0	0.0	0.0
34.	LAKSHADWEEP	1	1.6	0.0	0	0.0	0.0	0	0.0	0.0	0	0.0	0.0
35.	PONDICHERRY	56	5.6	0.2	27	2.7	0.2	0	0.0	0.0	0	0.0	0.0
TOTAL (UTs)		**573**	**3.3**	1.7	**138**	**0.8**	**1.1**	**0**	**0.0**	0.0	**0**	**0.0**	**0.0**
TOTAL (ALL-INDIA)		**32939**	**3.1**	**100.0**	**12325**	**1.2**	**100.0**	**46**	**0.0**	**100.0**	**0**	**0.0**	**0.0**

Table 3.3 : *(Contd...)*

Sl. No.	*State / UT*	*Immoral Traffic (P) Act*			*Indecent Representation of Women (P) Act*			*Dowry Prohibition Act*			*Total*		
		I	*R*	*P*	*I*	*R*	*P*	*I*	*R*	*P*	*I*	*R*	*P*
(1)	*(2)*	*(28)*	*(29)*	*(30)*	*(31)*	*(32)*	*(33)*	*(34)*	*(35)*	*(36)*	*(37)*	*(38)*	*(39)*
States													
1.	ANDHRA PRADESH	349	0.4	6.3	909	1.2	87.2	195	0.3	7.3	18382	23.6	13.1
2.	ARUNACHAL PRADESH	0	0.0	0.0	0	0.0	0.0	0	0.0	0.0	139	12.3	0.1
3.	ASSAM	22	0.1	0.4	0	0.0	0.0	92	0.3	3.4	5312	19.2	3.8
4.	BIHAR	9	0.0	0.2	1	0.0	0.1	706	0.8	26.3	5900	6.8	4.2
5.	CHHATTISGARH	7	0.0	0.1	0	0.0	0.0	16	0.1	0.6	3336	15.4	2.4
6.	GOA	25	1.8	0.5	0	0.0	0.0	0	0.0	0.0	121	8.5	0.1
7.	GUJARAT	74	0.1	1.3	14	0.0	1.3	0	0.0	0.0	5735	10.9	4.1
8.	HARYANA	57	0.3	1.0	0	0.0	0.0	3	0.0	0.1	4170	18.9	3.0
9.	HIMACHAI PRADESH	5	0.1	0.1	0	0.0	0.0	7	0.1	0.3	729	11.7	0.5
10.	JAMMU & KASHMIR	2	0.0	0.0	0	0.0	0.0	4	0.0	0.1	2164	20.2	1.5
11.	JHARKHAND	6	0.0	0.1	0	0.0	0.0	261	0.9	9.7	2488	8.9	1.8
12.	KARNATAKA	1361	2.5	24.7	0	0.0	0.0	341	0.6	12.7	5834	10.7	4.1
13.	KERALA	159	0.5	2.9	16	0.0	1.5	4	0.0	0.1	5653	17.3	4.0
14.	MADHYA PRADESH	33	0.1	0.6	0	0.0	0.0	29	0.0	1.1	14547	23.0	10.3
15.	MAHARASHTRA	179	0.2	3.2	8	0.0	0.8	29	0.0	1.1	11273	11.2	8.0
16.	MANIPUR	0	0.0	0.0	0	0.0	0.0	0	0.0	0.0	137	5.5	0.1
17.	MEGHALAYA	1	0.0	0.0	0	0.0	0.0	0	0.0	0.0	69	2.9	0.0
18.	MIZORAM	0	0.0	0.0	0	0.0	0.0	0	0.0	0.0	147	15.9	0.1
19.	NAGALAND	1	0.0	0.0	0	0.0	0.0	0	0.0	0.0	25	1.2	0.0
20.	ORISSA	11	0.0	0.2	0	0.0	0.0	412	1.1	15.4	4946	13.1	3.5
21.	PUNJAB	54	0.2	1.0	1	0.0	0.1	3	0.0	0.1	2375	9.5	1.7
22.	RAJASTHAN	51	0.1	0.9	87	0.1	8.3	3	0.0	0.1	11812	19.9	8.4

(Contd...)

Table 3.# : *(Contd...)*

(1)	(2)	(28)	(29)	(30)	(31)	(32)	(33)	(34)	(35)	(36)	(37)	(38)	(39)
23.	SIKKIM	1	0.2	0.0	0	0.0	0.0	0	0.0	0.0	37	6.6	0.0
24.	TAMIL NADU	2839	4.5	51.5	6	0.0	0.6	175	0.3	6.5	8888	14.0	6.3
25.	TRIPURA	0	0.0	0.0	0	0.0	0.0	0	0.0	0.0	537	16.3	0.4
26.	UTTAR PRADESH	47	0.0	0.9	0	0.0	0.0	367	0.2	13.7	12840	7.4	9.1
27.	UTTARANCHAL	0	0.0	0.0	0	0.0	0.0	1	0.0	0.0	886	10.0	0.6
28.	WEST BENGAL	152	0.2	2.8	1	0.0	0.1	17	0.0	0.6	8508	10.3	6.1
TOTAL (STATES)		**5445**	**0.5**	**98.8**	**1043**	**0.1**	**100.0**	**2665**	**0.3**	**99.3**	**136990**	**13.0**	**97.4**
29.	A & N ISLANDS	0	0.0	0.0	0	0.0	0.0	0	0.0	0.0	22	5.9	0.0
30.	CHANDIGARH	4	0.4	0.1	0	0.0	0.0	0	0.0	0.0	159	16.6	0.1
31.	D & N HAVELI	2	0.9	0.0	0	0.0	0.0	0	0.0	0.0	13	5.6	0.0
32.	DAMAN & DIU	0	0.0	0.0	0	0.0	0.0	0	0.0	0.0	10	6.0	0.0
33.	DELHI	46	0.3	0.8	0	0.0	0.0	14	0.1	0.5	3282	22.1	2.3
34.	LAKSHADWEEP	0	0.0	0.0	0	0.0	0.0	0	0.0	0.0	4	6.3	0.0
35.	PONDICHERRY	13	1.3	0.2	0	0.0	0.0	5	0.5	0.2	121	12.0	0.1
TOTAL (UTs)		**65**	**0.4**	**1.2**	**0**	**0.4**	**0.0**	**19**	**0.1**	**0.7**	**3611**	**20.5**	**2.6**
TOTAL (ALL-INDIA)		**5510**	**0.5**	**100.0**	**1043**	**0.1**	**100.0**	**2684**	**0.3**	**100.0**	**140601**	**13.2**	**100.0**

Some Facts and Figures related to Crime Against Women

Around the World

- One in five women will be a victim of rape or attempted rape in her lifetime. (*WHO, 1997*)
- In South Africa 147 women are raped every day. (*South African Institute for Race Relations, 2003*).
- In the USA a woman is raped every 90 seconds. (*US Department of Justice, 2000*)
- In France 25,000 women are raped per year. (*European Women's Lobby, 2001*)
- In Turkey 35.6 per cent of women have experienced marital rape sometimes and 16.3 per cent often. (Surveys published in 2000, *Women and Sexuality in Muslim Societies,* WWHR Publications: Istanbul, 2000)

Women and War

Violence against women during conflict has reached epidemic proportions. Mass rape is frequently used systematically, as a weapon of war. On top of this, during conflict women are physically and economically forced to become prostitutes, sometimes in order to secure the basic necessities for their families. War impacts on women in other ways—women and children are also the majority of refugees and internally displaced persons.

Around the World

- 80 per cent of the refugees are women and children. (*UNHCR, 2001*)
- Millions of women and children are caught in 34

communal, ethnic, political and/or international armed conflicts around the world [all active instances of societal armed conflicts as of 1st January, 2003. CSP) Centre for Systemic Peace]

- Trafficking of women and girls was reported in 85 per cent of the conflict zones. (*We the Children, 2003*)
- In the Democratic Republic of Congo 5,000 cases of rape, corresponding to an average of 40 a day, were recorded in the Uvira area by women associations since October 2002. (*UN, 2003*)
- In Rwanda between 250,000 and 500,000 women, or about 20 per cent of Women, were raped during the 1994 genocide. (*International Red Cross Report, 2002*)
- In Sierra Leone 94 per cent of displaced households surveyed had experienced sexual assaults, including rape, torture and sexual slavery. (*Physicians for Human Rights, 2002*)
- In Iraq at least 400 women and girls as young as eight were reported to have been raped in Baghdad during or after the war, since April 2003. (*Human Rights Watch Survey, 2003*)
- Every 14 days a Colombian woman is a victim of forced "disappearance" according to a 2001 Report by the Women and Armed Conflict Work Table. (*UNIFEM, 2001*)
- Approximately 250,000 Cambodian women were forced into marriage between 1975 and 1979. On average, two group marriages may have taken place in every Cambodian village during the Khmer Rouge Regime (UNIFEM).
- In Bosnia and Herzegovina 20,000 to 50,000 women were raped during five months of conflict in 1992. (*IWTC, Women's Global Net #212. 23rd October, 2002*)

- In some villages in Kosovo, 30 per cent to 50 per cent of women of child bearing age were raped by Serbian forces. (*Amnesty International, 27th May, 1999*)

Harmful Practices

Virtually every culture in the world contains forms of violence against women that are nearly invisible because they are seen as "normal" or "customary".

Around the World

- More than 135 million girls and women have undergone female genital mutilation and an additional 2 million girls and women are at risk each year (6,000 every day). (*A, UN, 2002*)
- 82 million girls who are now aged 10 to 17 will be married before their 18th birthday. (*UNFP*)
- In more than 28 countries in Africa, female genital mutilation is practised. (*Amnesty International, 1997*)
- In Niger 76 per cent of the poorest young women will marry before the age of 18. (*UNFPA, 2003*)
- 97 per cent of married women in Egypt aged 15 to 49 have undergone female genital mutilation. (*WHO Survey, 1996*)
- In Iran 45 women under the age of 20 years have been murdered in so-called "honour" killings by close relatives in Iran's majority ethnic Arab province of Khuzestan in a two-month period in 2003. (*Middle East Times, 31st October, 2003*)
- Female genital mutilation has been reported in Asian countries such as India, Indonesia, Malaysia and Sri Lanka as well as among immigrant communities in Australia. (*UN, 2002*)

- In India there are close to 15,000 dowry deaths estimated per year. Mostly they are kitchen fires designed to look like accidents. (*Injustices Studies, Vol. 1, November, 1997*)
- Female genital mutilation is performed amongst immigrant communities in Denmark, France, Italy, the Netherlands, Sweden, Switzerland and the United Kingdom. (*UN, 2002*)

The State Failing Victims of Violence against Women

Violence against women goes widely unreported. There are various factors which prevent women from reporting incidents of violence, such as fear of retribution, lack of economic means, emotional dependence, concern for children and no access to redress. Few countries have special training for the police, judicial and medical staff to deal with rape cases.

Around the World

- Around 20-70 per cent of abused women never told another person about the abuse until being interviewed for the study by WHO. (*WHO, Geneva, 2002*)
- In South Africa the conviction rate for rape remains low at an average of 7 per cent. A third of the estimated number or rapes were reported in 2003. (*Police Annual Report for the Year ending March, 2003*)
- In Egypt 47 per cent of physically abused women never told anyone. (*Population-based study, 1999) (WHO, 2002*)
- In Chile only 3 per cent of all raped women report the incident to the police. (*WHO, 2002*)
- In the USA, 16 per cent of women report rapes to the police; of those who do not, nearly 50 per cent of women would do so if they could be assured that their names and private details would not be released

publicly. (*National Victim Centre/Crime Victims Research and Treatment Centre, 1992*)

- In Australia 18 per cent of women who were physically assaulted in a period of 12 months never told any one. (*Population-based Study, 1999*)
- In Bangladesh, 68 per cent of women never told anyone about being beaten. (*WHO, 2002*)
- In Austria, 20 per cent of reported rape cases ended in convictions in the 1990s. (*London Metropolitan University, 2003*)
- In Ireland, 20 per cent of physically abused women contacted the police. (*Population-based Study, 1999; WHO, 2002*)
- In the Russian Federation, 40 per cent of women victims of violence within the family do not seek help from law enforcement officials. (*International Helsinki Federation for Human Rights, Women, 2000: Russia*)
- In the United Kingdom, 13 per cent of all raped women report the assault to the police. (*Joni Seager, 2003*)

Violence with Impunity

Violence against women often remains unchecked and unpunished. Some states have no laws at all, others have flawed laws, which may punish some forms of violence but exempt others. Even with the appropriate legislation in place, many states fail to implement the law fully.

Around the World

- In 2003 at least, 54 countries had discriminatory laws against women. (based on a report by the *UN Special Rapporteur on Violence Against Women*).
- In her 1994-2003 review, the UN Special Rapporteur

on Violence Against Women highlighted problems of law enforcement in almost all of the reviewed states.

- 79 countries have no (or unknown) legislation against domestic violence (UNIFEM, Not a Minute More, 2003)
- Marital rape is recognized specifically as a crime in only 51 countries as far as information was available. (*UNIFEM, 2003*)
- Only 16 nations have legislation specifically referring to sexual assault, while as few as three have legislation that specifically addresses violence against women as a category of criminal activity in itself (Bangladesh, Sweden and USA). (*UNIFEM, 2003*)
- So called "honour" defences (partial or complete) are found in the penal codes of Peru, Bangladesh, Argentina, Ecuador, Egypt, Guatemala, Iran, Israel, Jordan, Syria, Lebanon, Turkey, the West Bank and Venezuela. (*UN, 2002*)

HIV/AIDS

Increasingly, violence against women is recognized as a major public health concern. Violence can affect woman's reproductive health as well as other aspects of her physical and mental well-being. Sexual violence against women has led to higher infection rates of HIV/AIDS than among men of the same age group.

Around the World

- 51 per cent of all people living with HIV/AIDS today (over 20 million) are women. (*UNIFEM, 2003*)
- Worldwide, over half of new HIV infections are occurring among young people between the ages of 15 to 24, and over 60 per cent of HIV-positive youth

between the ages of 15-24 are women. (*UNAIDS, 2003*)

- 5 per cent of the 16,000 new infections occurring daily are women. (*UNAIDS, 2003*)
- AIDS now ranks as one of the leading causes of death among women aged 20 to 40 in several cities in Europe, sub-Saharan Africa and North America. (*UNAIDS, 2003*)
- Three million died of AIDs - related illnesses in 2003. (*UNAIDS, 2003*)

* *Source:* Amnesty International, London.

References

Agarwal, Sushila, *Status of Women:* Printwell Publishers, Jaipur, 1988.

Ahuja, Ram, *Crime Against Women*, Rawat Publications, Jaipur.

Altekar, A.S., *Position of Women in Hindu Civilization*, Motilal Banarsi Das, 1938.

Antoy, M.J. *Women's Rights;* Dialogue Publication, New Delhi, 1985.

Archer, J and Lloyd, *B., Sex and Gender;* Harmonds - Worth, Penguin, 1982.

Archor, M.S., *Women Society and Change:* McGraw Hill Boom Company, New York, 1971.

Asthana, Pratima, *Women's Movement in India,* New Delhi, Vikas Publications, 1974.

Baig, Tara Ali, *India's Women Powers : S.*Chand &Co. Pvt. Ltd., - New Delhi, 1976.

Ais Human Resource in 21st Century and Beyond (Volume 4, Women and Globalisation): Sarup & Sons, New Delhi. 2001.

Bandwick, Judith, M. *Women in Transition;* The Harvest Press Ltd., Susses, 1980.

Boserup, Ester, *Women's Role in Economic Development,* St. Martin's Press, New York, 1970.

Chattopadhayay, Kanladwi, *Indian Women's Battle for Freedom;* Abhinav Publications, New Delhi, 1983.

Chanana, Karuna, *Socialisation, Education and Women,* Orient Publications, New Delhi, 1985.

Chapman, Jane Roberts, *Economic Independence of Women,* Sage Publications, London, 1976.

Crime in India, National Crime Records Bureau, Ministry of Home Affairs, Government of India, New Delhi, Annual Reports – 1998-2002.

Cormack, Margaret, *The Hindu Women,* New York, 1953.

Dak, T.M., *Women and Work in Indian Society,* Discovery Publishing House, Delhi, 1988.

Desai, Nena, *Women in Modern India,* Vohra & Co. Publishers Pvt. Ltd., Bombay, 1957.

Desai, Nena and Maithregi, Krishna Raj, *Women and Society in India,* Ajanta Publications, Delhi, 1987.

Devi, S, *Women's Status and Social Change:* Pointer Publishers, Jaipur, 1999.

Fleming, *Stopping Wife Abuse,* Doubtday, New York, 1979.

Gells, Richard J, *Family Violence,* Sage Publications, New Bury, 1987.

Ghosh, S.K. *Women in a Changing Society,* Ashish Publishing House, New Delhi, 1984.

Hate, Chandrakala A. Changing Status of Women in Post Independence India; Allied Publishers, Bombay, 1969.

Kaushik, Sushila, *Women's Oppression- Patterns and Perspectives:* Shakti Books, Vikas, New Delhi, 1985.

Karlekar, Malavika, *Poverty and Women's Work,* Vikas Publishing House, New Delhi, 1982.

Majumdar, Maya - *Protecting our Women,* Dominant Publishers and Distributors - New Delhi, 2001.

Maurya, S.D., *Women in India,* Chug Publications, Allahabad, 1988.

Mittal, Mukta, Woman Power in India; Anmol Pub., New Delhi, 1995.

Seth, Mira : *Women and Development. The Indian Experience :* Sage Publications, New Delhi, 2001.

Srinivas, M.N. *Changing Position of Indian Women,* Oxford University Press, New Delhi, 1978.

Srivastava. T.N., *Women and the Law,* Intellectual Publishing House, 1985.

Verma, H.N. and Amrit, *Women through the Ages,* Indian Publishers, New Delhi, 1976.

Yaqin, Anwarul and Anwar, Badar, *Protection of Women under Law; An Annotated Bibliography*: Deep & Deep Publications, New Delhi, 1982.

4

Feminization of Crime

A Legal Interrogation of Critical Criminology

Tapan R. Mohanty

In recent times the troubles and travails encountered by women in life and the subsequent discrimination and often dehumanizing experiences have arrested not only the attention of academicians, but lawmakers and politicians as well thus, engendering the contours of everyday discourse if not substantially enveloping it. Though the subjugation of women and their subjection to pervasive male ego finds its mention in 'Vindication of Rights of Women' way back in late eighteenth century only in last few decades it became a subject matter of serious discussion. The transition of gender studies from the margins to the mainline of academic sphere and consequently from the dark alleys of self-doubt to the podiums of world forums the journey though remarkable is full of vicious turns, dangerous twirls and of unflinching determination. The bulking bag of books and libraries of literature on women's studies are testimony to that struggle and triumph but rarely attempts have been made to provide the trials and tribulation of women as victims of crime from a combination of sociology, criminology and law and thereby putting this important debate into perspective. It is believed that criminology and sociology of deviance must become more than the study of men and crime if it is to play any significant part in the development of our understanding of crime, law, criminal process and play any role in the transformation of existing social practices (Smart, 1976). In this chapter an attempt has been made to look women as the victims of crime, problems of such a social context, the efforts to curb these atrocities and their contemporary relevance.

Crime is a complex phenomenon and it is a Herculean task to define and delineate crime in all its complexities and contexts. In the lexicon of criminal law crime is defined as 'an act capable of being followed by criminal proceedings having one of the types of outcomes (punishment, etc.) known to follow these proceedings (Kenny, 1936). Classical criminologists have defined crime in terms of absence of pity and probity (Garofalo) and those who followed them tried to find the proverbial 'criminal man' in deficiencies in physical traits, environmental and climatic conditions, social structure and in economic background. The debate dates back to the old Greek controversy of the fifth century B.C. between those who saw everything determined by nature and those who pressed the claims of convention on human legislation. To Aristotle we may trace the classical distinction between those acts which are crimes by nature (*mala per se*) and are prohibited among all peoples, and those others (*mala prohibita*) which are prohibited only in certain places by special legislation.

The later conceptualization of crime though took a multidisciplinary colour is often enmeshed in legalistic connotations. However, as the study of sociology have shown us that crime, criminal and criminality cannot be taken as isolated objects rather they need to be studied in their social context and along with other related social phenomena. Durkheimnian conceptualization of crime as a 'social fact' and more importantly as 'normal' was a result of critical thinking that understood deviance from accepted social standards as not only an expression of defiance of the norms but also points out the failures of the set paradigms. Examined from this perspective crime then provides an opportunity to understand the existing loopholes in the system and problems of the mindset that prey on the vulnerability of others and justifies acts of violence from retrograde and obsolete norms. Crime against women must be studied from this vantage point that underlines the deficiencies of the system and difficulties of women living under such threats.

Positivist, sociologist and jurists as well as moralists often identify crime with acts which are contrary to the social interests or endanger social existence. But the most obvious reflection shows that this begs the question. Acts are criminal not because they are harmful, but because they are deemed harmful by those who make or interpret law. The most serious crimes are sometimes those acts that in the judgment of enlightened and heroically unselfish people will best promote the common good.

In the past most heinous crimes have been the sacrilege or ceremonial defilement, witchcraft and heresy. Doubtless these were regarded with terror because they were supposed to endanger society by bringing down the wrath of gods who are not careful to discriminate between the guilty and innocent when they send down their lightening or diseases. But what they any community regards as most dangerous is not eternally fixed in the nature of things, but varies from time to time and from locality to locality in ways which we cannot always explain.

The chief concern of the criminal law is seriously anti-social behaviour. But the notion that English criminal law is only concerned with serious anti-social acts must be abandoned as one considers the broader canvas of criminal liability. There are many offences for which any element of stigma is diluted almost to vanishing point (Ashworth, 1995).

Based on the diversity of crimes and their context as well as the nature of crime it is extremely difficult to put together a theory of crime detailing the general characteristics. However, a close scrutiny of various definitions of crime suggests that a particular form of behaviour cannot be called criminal unless the following elements are present.

First, before behaviour can be called crime there must be certain external consequences or 'harm'. A crime has always a harmful impact on society, therefore, a crime against an individual is considered as crime against the society and the state. Secondly, the harm must be legally forbidden, must have been proscribed by penal law. There are many activities which are apparently against the morality and society yet they are not crime unless specifically prohibited by law, viz., lying, alcoholism, gambling, prostitution, etc. Third, there must be 'conduct'; that is, there must be an intentional or reckless action or inaction which brings the harmful consequence. However, action or inactions under duress and threat do not belong to this category as they are influenced by an external agency. Fourth, an act can be categorized as criminal when there is a 'criminal intent' on the part of the offender. An intention, however, needs to be distinguished from motive. There are instances where the motive is good but the intention is criminal. Fifth, there must be a concurrence of criminal intent and conduct. A fatal punch in a boxing match does not usually amount to homicide even though there is an action and apparently the intention to beat the opponent. Sixth, there must be a 'causal' relationship between the legally forbidden harm and the voluntary misconduct. In the absence of this causal relationship it becomes difficult to prove the crime and probably is the major reason where criminals often go scot-free after committing a crime. Notable among is the case of physical assault of women and child abuse when it takes longer to establish the chain of events. Seventh, there must be a legally prescribed punishment. It is not sufficient to proscribe the misconduct by law but also carry a threat of punishment to violators. However, these descriptions are only analytical and heuristic in nature and in a particular form of crime there may be some elements are present while few are missing as crimes are often judged by the context and the conduct. There are many exceptions to these features as well, for example, in case of sexual harassment the act itself is punishable and need not be interpolated with the intention. Similarly, in 'strict liability' cases the intention of the offender is not considered and he is liable to punishment simple because of the harmful consequences of his act.

Feminist Approach to Criminology

Though there have been sporadic efforts to examine crime and criminality through the lens of gender it only received wider attention in the event of second wave of feminism that focused on juxtaposing a woman's perspective of crime different from that of men's experience and reasoning. In 1961, criminologist Walter C. Reckless (1961) questioned whether any theory of delinquency would be accepted if a criminologist paused to consider if it applied to women. It was nearly a decade later, however, before Bernard (1969) and Heidensohn (1968) drew attention to the 'omission of women from general theories of crime' and 'signalled an awakening of criminology from its androcentric slumber' (Daly and Chesney-Lind 1988 : 507). Indeed, in hindsight the discovery of women as a conceptual term that could be incorporated into criminological theory has been called 'quite literally, pioneering' (Young 1992 : 289).

In a critique of mainstream criminology and its preoccupation with men's world Heidensohn noted, 'the patterns....of male and of female deviance were long observed,....nevertheless, the focus of research has been very much away from this particular area' (1968 : 160-61). In a different context Jefferson and Shapland wrote that 'feminism was the growth area in criminology....and now has a very powerful presence in the field... However .... One can argue that despite the massive growth about women, crime and law and criminal justice....the experience of women remained marginal to the criminological enterprise (1994 : 282).

Most of the criminological research, however, focused on two themes namely; the female offender and the experience of women prisoners. At the first instance, the shoplifting, drug addiction, prostitution were studied as crimes committed by women and the second one was an effort to draw a parallel between the experiences of male and female convicts and accused in the stigmatized space of prison, their collective trauma and ability to coalescence with outside world—its facts and features. Some of these studies had an obvious victim oriented perspective while others were intended to create awareness about the con woman.

The growth of capitalism and the journey to the post-modern world created a different sort of opportunity for the study of gender centric criminology. The concern for victims, rise of public interest litigation, movement to provide access to justice, the notion of exclusion spurred the need to have comprehensive and combined study of criminology by the state, police officials and criminologist. It was essential as the dimensions and directions of crime grew manifold and new experiences and meanings were carved out of precise acts of crime and from scenes of crime. In order to put things into perspective Garland has noted that 'older social welfare criminology ..... which views criminality as the dispositional outcome of social deprivation now compete with two new criminologies — of 'everyday life' and 'the other' (Garland 2001:182-4). As a result of such changes the gender and feminist issues have become the cutting edge of criminology, central and open to 'theoretical and methodological innovation' (Daly, 1997 : 42).

Crime, Critical Theory and Human Rights

The idea of crime being a morally constructed category is found in critical and conflict theories. Indeed, 'whether one is talking about crime as a violation of human rights, as a social harm, or a social injury, each of these definitions can be characterized as moral ones' (Barak, 1997). However, rather than being representative of an existing moral order, the approach is suggesting a humanitarian view of change. "The notion of crime as social injury, social harm, or violation of human rights, is in effect, basic to those who strive to improve the human condition, for it provides the intellectual and practical tools for the reconstruction of society" (Quinney and Wildeman, 1991 : 5).

An important difference, however, between the consensus theorists and those holding a pluralist/conflict position is the different concern shown to expand the number of dimensions of inclusion. In terms of our analytical schema critical modernists move away from the extremes of generalized victim categories, individual, state and society, and instead dramatically expand the number and variety of particularistic categories that are subject to harm. These include the underclass, women, racial and ethnic groups, sexual preferences, employees, professionals, people with disabilities, people with AIDS, etc., (Henry and Milovanovic, 1996 : 105). For example, Schwendinger and Schwendinger's (1970) notion of crime as a violation of human rights relates not just to human rights in general, but to crimes against specific groups including exploited classes, oppressed groups, and those who dominated because of race or gender.

Pluralist, conflict, critical and modernists have also drawn attention to crimes of repression and expand the number of dimensions beyond the traditional property, person and state to include social/ prestige and political standing, human rights, crimes against racism, patriarchal oppression, hate, invasion of privacy and autonomy, humiliation and harassment, etc. Crimes here are not only a reduction of a certain class or group standing but also a restriction, limitation, repression or prevention of that group or its members changing their relative standing (Henry and Milovanovic, 1996 : 106). In nutshell feminism is a range of committed inquiry and activity dedicated to (i) understand the extent of women's subordination, (ii) know the reasons, therefore, and (iii) plan and implement means of change for their better life (Dalton, 1987). Following the post-modern paradigm of focusing on the 'marginal' and looking at the 'criminalization of the conduct' of the 'others' and 'victimization' of the 'different' in this section an attempt has been made to map the territory of trauma of the victims of 'human rights violations' in general and women in particular. Violence is gendered, embodied (Thapan, 1997) and institutionalized. Feminists, for long, have been trying to depict that male violence is integral to patriarchal social order (Brownmiller, 1976; Hanmer and Saunders, 1984; Walby, 1990; Mackninnon, 1997).

Over the last decade or so, the phrase 'women's rights as human rights' has been used to explore, assert and redress the gap between the stated international commitment to equality for women and the actual experience of women (Bell, 1999). But very little has been done in the face of wider disparities that exist among various women groups culturally and socially. As a result one can perceive vast differences in the cognitive, connotative and consumption pattern of women residing in various spheres of social and economic layers. The victims of exploitation and oppression have been largely the women of third world countries in general and the lower section among them in particular.

One of the key aspects of religious fundamentalism is its tendency to take political action aimed at conforming a state's (country's) law to religious doctrine, particularly in areas affecting women's rights (Howland, 1997). Fundamentalists are particularly concerned with women's sexuality—as a danger and as a threat to society—and thus are keen to regulate and control women's sexuality and reproduction through a variety of measures. Controlling women's sexuality fits neatly into the religious fundamentalists promotion of the patriarchal family and the 'proper' role for women as being in the home. A feature that fundamentalisms share is an emphasis on women's role being confined to that of wife and mother and the restriction of their role in the public world. (Howland, 1999).

Cultural Relativism and Universal Human Rights

With respect to certain discriminatory religious laws that have not been enacted into state law, the state has an affirmative obligation to provide effective legal remedies for women abused under these laws and to protect its citizens against certain actions that have hereafter been characterized as 'private', Such state action is the only way to guarantee women's political freedom's such that they can be fully effective citizens in a democratic polity.

Human beings in many places and at many times have searched for a universal sense of truth, values, ethics, morality and justice. Relativism is the view that this search is hopeless and futile because the concepts of truth and falsehood, right and wrong, rights and duties, can exist and be valid only within a specific context that defines them and gives them meaning, and consequently they can have no universal validity. Cultural relativists define the 'culture of the group in various ways, but generally in terms of a supposedly shared group process by which meaning is assigned to behaviour, social action is articulated, and social modes for guiding and governing behaviour are developed, (Geertz, 1973). In many cultures, women live within their own structural forms and derive their normative sense from them. The international community, following anthropology, has tended to ignore such lines of separation even when the separation reaches the level of segregation. But if women and men in such a group develop discernibly different senses of meaning and norms, then we might just as well identify two cultures within the group, within many cases, one culture at least in part dominating the other (Tylor, 1987).

The right to self-determination has also been linked to that of democratic entitlement, (Frank, 1992) but the formal processes of western democracy assumed to be part of democratic entitlement typically deliver less freedom to women than to men. It is important to know that women's status in society-socially, politically, legally, economically has been fundamentally the same across history for a majority of the world's population. Except for surface differences in manner and style, the basic arrangements for division of labour and power between men and women have been the same across the world. A woman's right over major decisions about her children's future, place of residence, marriage, inheritance, employment, and the like have been severely curtailed in most of the world during most of human history (Huddard and Banks, 1985).

The international community now recognizes that women's rights are human rights and human rights are women rights.

From the Vienna Declaration and Programme of Action, part I, para. 18 :

> "The human rights of women and of the girl-child are an inalienable, integral and indivisible part of universal human rights. The full and equal participation of women in political, civil, economic, social and cultural life, at the national, regional and international levels, and the eradication of all forms of discrimination on grounds of sex are priority objectives of the international community."

Excerpts from Discrimination Against Women : The Convention and the Committee, Fact Sheet No. 22, UN Centre for Human Rights :

> "Equality is the cornerstone of every democratic society which aspires to social justice and human rights. In virtually all societies and spheres of activity women are subject to inequalities in law and in fact. This situation is both caused and exacerbated by the existence of discrimination in the family, in the community and in the workplace. While causes and consequences may vary from country to country, discrimination against women is widespread. It is perpetuated by the survival of stereotypes and of traditional cultural and religious practices and beliefs detrimental to women....
>
> "The concept of equality means much more than treating all persons in the same way....True equality can only emerge from efforts directed towards addressing and correcting ... situational imbalances. It is this broader view of equality which has become the underlying principle and the final goal in the struggle for recognition and acceptance of the human rights of women...."

These positions are recorded in several international documents, and are encapsulated by the mission statement to the platform for Action of the United Nation's Fourth World Conference on Women held in Beijing, 1995. The platform for Action is an agenda for women's empowerment .... This means that the principle of shared power and responsibility should be established between women and men at home, in the workplace and in the wider national and international communities. Equality between women and men is a matter of human rights and condition for social justice and is also necessary and fundamental prerequisite for equality, development and peace. A transformed partnership based on equality between women and men is a condition for people centred sustainable development. A sustained and long-term commitment is essential, so that women and men can work together for themselves, for their children and for society to meet the challenges of the twenty-first century. Most of the cultural practices that apperently violate women's human rights relate to the control of female sexuality (Coomaraswamy, 1994).

Female genital mutilation is perhaps the best-known example. Human rights instruments drafted by men are silent on the issue of sexuality and reproductive rights. Feminist legal scholars have attempted to read these rights so that a woman's physical integrity is respected with regard to her reproductive organs (Cook, 1995). Here the term "reproductive health paradigm" refer to a view of reproductive and sexual health and rights that found its fullest — even if still imperfect official, public expression in the declaration and programmes that emerged from the ICPD and the Fourth World Conference on Women held in Beijing in 1995. The ICPD programme, in particular, can be seen as the culmination of more than a decade of work by women's movements throughout the world, coming from different perspectives and situations, and building on many years of local activism on women's health and right issues.

The Convention on the Elimination of All Forms of Discrimination Against Women ... sets out, in legally binding form, internationally accepted principles on the rights of women which are applicable to all women.... The basic legal norm of the Convention is the prohibition of all forms of discrimination against women. This norm cannot be satisfied merely by the enactment of gender-neutral laws. In addition to demanding that women be accorded equal rights with men, the Convention goes further by prescribing the measures to be taken to ensure that women everywhere are able to enjoy the rights to which they are entitled. "The Convention was adopted by the General Assembly in 1979 to reinforce the provisions of existing international instruments ... designed to combat the continuing discrimination against women. It identifies many specific areas where there has been notorious discrimination against women, for example in regard to political rights, marriage and the family, and employment. In these and other areas the Convention spells out specific goals and measures that are to be taken to facilitate the creation of a global society in which women enjoy full equality with men and thus full realization of their guaranteed human rights."

Women and Crime in India

Contemporary theme of feminist criminology is the 'pervasiveness of male dominance in patriarchal society and its impact on crimes committed both by and against women (Akers, 1994). Despite the shifting of focus from omission of women from theory to the emancipation of women from the crime, the methodology of research continues to be on power relations. Marxist theories of crime focus, for instance, on the power of the ruling class, and most conflict theories focus on the conflict between various powerful and powerless groups. For feminist theory, men's power over women is the dominant theme (Lilly *et al.*, 1995 : 183). Even under democratic dispensation the power relations become quite apparent disturbing the fragile policies of gender equality. Women as free citizens, and constituting almost half of the population, are theoretically able to redress their grievances through democratic means. But due to socio-economic reasons and cultural patterns they are not effective players of the game of democracy. The disadvantages of democratic process and risks of parliamentary majoritarianism make it imperative that a pro-women and anti-subordination interpretation of Constitution and law is difficult to make. In a patriarchal social construction, where power dictates freedom, lack of power on the part of women because of their position as incomplete agents in democratic participation is likely to marginalize their freedom (Higgins, 1987).

Rape, other forms of sexual abuse including date and marital rape, and domestic violence each has been explained by patriarchal dominance. Again, these crimes by men — and thus the victimization of women — reflect the ability of men to use their power against women. The situation is not different in India rather quite alarming. Despite having a high tradition of respecting the dignity of women and recognizing their contribution to society women in India in general suffer from a variety of indignity and discrimination, notwithstanding the constitutional obligations. Within the home and outside the four walls of home women in India have been suppressed, oppressed and consigned to the status of a secondary citizen, often becoming victims of snide remarks and derision. The local culture, folktales and general condition of women are lurid reminder to the way they have been treated by their men folk. The practice of *sati*, female infanticide, *purdah* and dowry like many others exposes the discrimination that exists even today between two sexes irrespective of the historicity of these traditions. In Indian society women have always been vulnerable to all sorts of heinous crimes like domestic violence, sexual assault, sexual harassment at workplace, trafficking, female foeticide, etc.

Although crime against women constitute hardly 13.5 per cent of the total crimes committed in the country, yet both the range of such crimes and their absolute numbers are quite significant. Women are subjected to a plethora of violence throughout their lifecycle ranging from foeticide, infanticide, torture, rape, molestation, battering, trafficking, prostitution, forced marriage, dowry death, custodial violence, and so on. Violence against women is a reflection of the deep rooted 'gender bias' of the society. Often the crimes are committed by people who are close to the victims and are traditionally supposed to be their protectors, but the victims, especially the sexually abused girls continues to be tormented by the trauma, an act where the victim is penalized rather than the culprit.

Selected Crime against Women (1990-1998)

Crime	*1990*	*1994*	*1998*
Rape	10068	13208	15031
Dowry Deaths	13450	25956	41318
Cruelty by husband and relatives	4836	4935	6917

Source : Crime in India -1998, National Crime Records Bureau, Government of India, New Delhi.

But only a miniscule of violence committed against is covered under the legal provisions and the majority of them are unreported for various reasons. Even then the statistics unequivocally shows the increasing trend of violence against women. These violations are generated especially against poor, minorities and more in case of women. In a world rocked by violence, women face rape, mutilation and death at the hands of not only of common men but also of those in power including armed forces. They are beaten by their husbands, they are stripped by upper caste men, they are subjected to rape and finally left to die uncared for and unnoticed in a helpless society.

Select forms of Violence against Women

Sexual Abuse, Rape and Sexual Assault

The word 'abuse' has a very wide meaning, everything which is contrary to good order established by usage amounts to abuse. Physical or mental mal-treatment also is an abuse; an injury to genital organs is an attempt of sexual intercourse also amounts to sexual abuse. Forcing a woman into sexual relationship against her will or forcing her to watch certain sexual acts without her consent amounts to sexual abuse.

Physical attacks by a partner may include rape and sexual violence. Women in many societies, however, do not define forced sex as rape if they are married to, or living with the attacker. In recent times, however, some countries have recognized martial rape as a criminal offence. Each such incident results in violation of fundamental rights of the women. Although rape and sexual assault may be perpetrated by strangers, evidences from many sources indicate that a high percentage of rapists are acquaintances, friends, relatives and those in positions of power. Rape is the most heinous crime committed against women by a man which is often the result of the unequal power relations and perpetrated to achieve complete control over the victim and to subordinate her to male ego.

Female Foeticide and Infanticide

Female foetuses are killed even before they acquire the age of viability in mother's womb. The advancement of medical technology change the fate of unborn child and posed a threat to its life, in particular to life of female child in the form of foetus. In such a test, if a female foetus is found, it is terminated by a deliberate abortion. The female foeticide is increasing throughout India and alarmingly in the developed regions of the country.

Domestic Violence

To quote Virginia Wolf "On marriage, the weakest, the stupidest, the most insignificant man in the world receives a license to rape and beat".

Domestic violence includes all types of violence against women in matrimonial home. It includes abuses of all kinds: physical, psychological, sexual, economic, emotional and verbal. It includes denial of basic necessities and the additional emotional blackmail where there are children are concerned and the threat of dispossession from the matrimonial home. It is generally denying the woman her right as an individual, her freedom of choice and liberty of action.

Domestic violence in India has many aspects : apart from violence between spouses, there is violence between siblings, between the other cohabitees, abuse of children by parents and *vice versa*. Dowry related violence is a problem unique to India. It cuts across all background—be it social, cultural, economic or religious beyond the caste, class and ethnicity. Domestic violence is all about power relations and the abuse of power in a household. It is perpetrated by one member or members collectively on another to gain control. In India, majority of such crimes are committed by men, though it needs to be acknowledged that women too become partners in such an attempt.

Sexual Harassment at Workplace

Right to life means life with dignity. Gender equality includes protection from sexual harassment and right to work with dignity. As we have discussed earlier the CEDAW recommended various suggestions and principles to curb these practices often used by men as acts of pleasure and policy of dehumanization and subordination. Sexual harassment includes unwelcome determined behaviours such as physical contacts and advances, sexually coloured remarks, showing pornography and currying sexual demands either by words or by actions.

The Supreme Court in its historic judgment in the case of *Vishaka* v. *State of Rajasthan* (AIR 1997 SC 3011) took cognizance of the fact that for realizing the concept of gender equality it is necessary that sexual harassment of working women in all working places must be prevented. A working woman is exposed to various hazardous situations, which may lead to any kind of depravity. This may lead to violations of her rights guaranteed under articles of 14, 15, 19 and 21 of the Constitution.

Judicial Response to Crime against Women

An important approach to the study of law and gender in democratic nation-state is to look at the judicial interpretation and administration of justice in cases involving gender, discrimination, assault on modesty and dignity of women as well as other forms of crimes against women. The purposive interpretation of law tries to elicit and focus on the reason or spirit behind the constitutional provisions and law. By looking at the values of the right, social needs, competing interest and policy alternatives, the development of sociological jurisprudence expands the ambit of rights. For example, by analyzing that guarantee of right to life and personal liberty should enable development of human personality rather than continuance of animal existence, the court reasons that right to life means right to live with human dignity and all those interest essential to this constitute essential parts of this right :

(i) In order to conform the aspiration reflected in the term 'protection' in the marginal note to Article 21 it is essential to note that access to those conditions which makes life livable with human dignity is part of right under Article 21. If at workplace an atmosphere with potential for sexual harassment exists, positive responsibility of the state and employers to remove such atmosphere and create a sense of security is the method of protection. The term of 'protection' in the clause 'equal protection of the laws' under Article 14 as viewed by Granville Austin, "seems to place upon government the positive responsibility to give access to those rights they previously have been powerless to exercise" (Austin 1999 : 669). With an array of Directive Principles of State policy which has great relevance in women's welfare;

(ii) Purposive interpretation is a seminal tool for the cause of constitutional feminism. It is appropriate to see how the Indian constitutional experience evinces the working of constitutional feminism.

Article 21 of the Constitution does not use the term 'state' and this allows scrutiny of private actions that violates right to life and personal liberty. The mandate of Article 21 which prohibits deprivation of life and personal liberty except according to the procedure established law is applicable against all entities whether state or private. It is because, from the perspective of the victim, deprivation of the right by private person is also deprivation, and is to be justified strictly in accordance with law.

(iii) In Nilima Priyadarshini case, the apex Court exercised *habeas corpus* jurisdiction in an alleged case of detention of a woman by a private person.

(iv) In Nasrin, a notorious case of detention of a woman in brothel subsequent to her sale by her husband, the Court exercised the *habeas corpus* jurisdiction and got the woman released.

Supreme Court of India has been, for the last two decades, making many bold innovations in administering what may be called 'substantive justice' to women. Three of its recent judgments in the realm of 'gender justice' were (1) *Vishakha Vs. State of Rajasthan* (1997) 6 SCC 241; (2) *Apparel Export Promotion Council* Vs. *A. K. Chopra* (1999) 1 SCC 759 and (3) *Gita Hariharan* Vs. *Reserve Bank of India* (1999) 2 SCC 228. In all these cases, the Supreme Court invoked and strongly relied on the provisions of international instruments, ostensibly to fill the void in the domestic law. This represented a significant departure from the Court's earlier stand in keeping with the traditional rule as to the applicability of international instruments which unlike customary International Law, ordinarily, must go through 'the process of transformation into municipal laws', before becoming enforceable by the domestic courts.

(v) In *Vishakha* case the Court depicted feminist vision as a major for its reasoning based on Convention on Elimination of All forms of Discrimination against Women (CEDAW), Directive Principles of State Policy (DPSP), affirmative action policy under Article 15 (3) and the human rights jurisprudence. It is because of this vision that the extraordinary type of judicial law making in this case became non-controversial and acceptable. While Vishakha was a Class action, the more recent case of *Apparel Export Promotion Council* Vs. *A. K. Chopra* was an adversarial litigation. The employer AEPC has taken disciplinary action, leading to termination of service, against A. K. Chopra. He was a company officer who had been found guilty of causing sexual harassment to Mrs. X, a stenographer by making sexually coloured remarks and soliciting sexual intimacy, taking advantage of his superior position. By implication, he had caused Mrs. X to believe that her objection would be disadvantageous to her in her employment and adverse consequences might result if she did not consent to such advances or sought to resist the same. However, Chopra was directed to be reinstated in service by the High Court, being the first court of judicial review, on the ground that at the most he had only attempted to commit the offence but had not actually done it. When the matter was brought in appeal to the Supreme Court, the Court reacted sharply resulting in the dismissal of Chopra from the service.

(vi) In *Gita Hariharan* Vs. *Reserve Bank of India* case the issue was whether the mother of minor child could be regarded under the Guardianship statute, as the 'natural guardian' of the child when the father was alive. The statute law on the subject was to the effect that the natural guardian of a minor is 'the father and after him the mother'. This was always taken to mean that if the father was alive, he would be the natural guardian, and only after his death the mother can be the natural guardian. Supreme Court felt that such an interpretation would lead to unfair discrimination against the mother and would amount to breach of gender equality as guaranteed by the Constitution and international instruments. Therefore, Court read down the provision of the statute, and construed the words 'after him' following the word 'father' to mean, the mother would be the natural guardian even during the lifetime of the father, if the father was absent from the scene of the minor either due to his own indifference or by choice or when he was physically absent or when he was unable to perform the duties of guardianship for any disability or did not want to do, or when he had no objection to the mother being the guardian. Though this case did not lay down any principle regarding feminization of crime or crime against women but it did highlight the need to unchain women and their right from the clutches of patriarchal mindset.

In the lens of criminology as Mac Kinnon (1987) has pointed out gender must be viewed as hierarchy and not just a difference and argues that efforts to treat gender as a question of difference are misguided and that gender should be understood to be a matter of domination and subordination. In this context it may be examined that the difference which as analysis just satisfies the formalistic reasonable explanation about differences based on sex, dominance analysis look at the substantive issue of unfair disadvantages arising from dominance. Based on the multilayered patterns of diversity, distinction and difference a complex set of discriminatory practices emerge from society that encapsulates the entire gamut of woman's life, thus restricting her liberty and limiting her choices. These societal and cultural orientations have severely damaged the phenomenological and ontological existence of women and their participation in public and private sphere. Forced against the walls of antagonism, discrimination and deprivation women have weathered the storms of tyranny, oppression and crime even at the hands of protectors. Realizing these difficulties the latest Commission set up by the Union Government to look into the criminal justice system recommended following measures to safeguard the interest of women in an increasingly criminalized society.

Observations and Recommendations of Malimath Committee

Firstly, a woman in a second marriage is not entitled to claim maintenance as in law a second marriage during subsistence of the first marriage is not legal and valid. Such a woman though she is *de facto* the wife of the man in law she is not his wife. In fact, quite often the man marries the second wife suppressing the fact and evidence regarding the earlier marriage. In such a situation the second wife cannot claim the benefit of Section 125 of Criminal Procedure Code for no fault of hers. The husband is absolved of his responsibility of maintaining his second wife. This is a clear case where the victim is further victimized where offender roams free— a clear violation of the fundamental canons of criminal jurisprudence that boldly proclaims, 'let thousand guilty go scot-free but a single innocent should not be punished'.

Secondly, there is a general complaint that Section 498 A of the Indian Penal Code regarding cruelty by the husband or his relatives is subjected to gross misuse and many times operates against the interest of the wife herself. This offence is non-bailable and non-compoundable. Hence, husband and other members of the family are arrested and can be behind the bars which may result in the husband losing his job. Even if the wife is willing to condone and forgive the lapses of her husband and live in matrimony, this provision comes in the way of spouses returning to the matrimonial home.

In view of the above issues the Committee has given several recommendations some of which are given below :

> The Committee suggested that the definition of the word 'wife' in Section 125 of Cr.P.C. should be amended so as to include a woman who was living with the man as his wife for a reasonably long period, during the subsistence of first marriage.

Section 494 of Indian Penal Code be suitably amended to the effect that if the man and woman were living together as husband and wife for reasonably long period the man shall be deemed to have married the woman according to the customary rites of either party.

In the context of Section 498A of the Indian Penal Code the Committee recommended that the hardship can be avoided by making offences bailable and compoundable.

The Committee has also laid down its opinion in cases relating to non-penile penetration or object penetration and declared, that it was not in favour of keeping it under the ambit of 'rape' defined under Section 375 of IPC. It recommended that as such an offence by its very nature is extremely grave and lowers the dignity of women and, therefore, should be treated as a separate offence carrying a higher punishment broadly on the lines of Section 376 of the IPC.

Conclusion

In the context of above narration and analysis of the intricate relationship between crime, law and gender it would be pertinent to postulate that a systematic and collective effort is required to eradicate crime against women and, alleviate the sufferings of the fair sex. In order to create a just, equal and fair society which is ostensibly the ideal of human civilization we need to deal with gender disparity and discrimination in general and criminal justice system in particular. In a 'knowledge society' which has provided fabulous opportunities to women in enlightening their life through knowledge, information, education and enthuse their self with the fruits of modernity and empowerment, gender stereotyping and archetypical role allocation has neither relevance nor necessity. In fact, the economic opportunities available in the era of globalization and market capitalism requires additional trained and skilled hands and restricting the option of women in the labour market will not only hurt the economy of the nation-state but will deprive the generation from the benefits of equity and justice. It is great concern to note that many of the crimes against the women are offshoots of jealousy, a false sense of superiority, effort to kill competitiveness and employment insecurity and not to mention psychological and emotional instability. These coupled with archaic notions of male chauvinism had created a gulf between two complementary sets of gender. But this chasm cannot be bridged by either by law or sociology rather we must combine these two important disciplines and their cumulative strength with emphasis on Information, Education and Communication (IEC). This will certainly help us in avoiding the growing trend of feminization of crime.

Notes

Action of the United Nations' Fourth World Conference on Women held in Beijing, 1995

Apparel Export Promotion Council vs. A. K. Chopra (1999) 1 SCC 759.

Articles 14, 15, 19 and 21 of The Constitution of India.

Convention on the Elimination of All Forms of Discrimination Against Women (CEDAW)

Crime in India -1998, National Crime Records Bureau, Government of India, New Delhi.
Discrimination Against Women: The Convention and the Committee, Fact Sheet #22, UN Centre for Human Rights.
Directive Principles of State Policy, Part- III of Constitution of India, Articles 39 (a) to (f), 42, 43, 44, 45, 47 and 51.
Fourth World Conference on Women held in Beijing in 1995.
Francis Coralie Mullin *vs*. Administrator, Union Territory of Delhi, (1981) 1 SCC 608:1981 SCC (Cri) 212.
Gita Hariharan *vs*. Reserve Bank of India (1999) 2 SCC 228.
International Conference on Population and Development (1994).
Indian Express, 4th February, 1994 (Bangalore edition).
Malimath Committee Report.
Nilima Priyadarshini *vs*. State of Bihar, 1987 Supp. SCC 732 : 1988 SCC (Cri) 138 and 1989 Supp (i) SCC 336.
Section 125 of Criminal Procedure Code.
Sections 375, 376, 498A of the Indian Penal Code.
Vienna Declaration and Programme of Action, Part I, Para. 18.

References

Akers, R. L. (1994). *Criminological Theories : Introduction and Evaluation*, Los Angeles: Roxbury.
Allen, F. A. (1973). Raffaele Garofalo. In H. Mannheim (Ed.) *Pioneers in Criminology* (2 ed., pp.318-340). Montclair, NJ : Patterson Smith.
Aristotle, (1980). *The Nicomachean Ethics* (tr. David Ross). Oxford : Oxford University Press.
Ashworth, A. (1995). *Principles of Criminal Law,* 2nd Edition, Oxford Clarendon Press.
Austin, G. (1999). *Working of a Democratic Constitution : The Indian Experience*. New Delhi: Oxford University Press.
Barak, G. (1997). *Integrating Criminologies*. Boston : Allyn and Bacon.
Bell, C. (1999). 'Women's Rights as Human Rights : Old Agendas in New Guises', in *Human Rights: An Agenda for 21st Century*. A. Hegarty and S. Leonard (eds.), London : Cavendish Publishing Limited.
Bernard, M. A. (1969). Self-image and Delinquency : A contribution to the study of female criminality and women's image. *Acta*

Criminologia : Etudes sur la Conduitor Antisociale, 2, 71-144 (Quoted in Lilly *et al.*)

Braithwaite, J. (1969). *Crime, Shame and Reintegration*. Cambridge, UK: Cambridge University Press.

Brownmiller, S. (1975). *Against our will : Men, Women and Rape*. New York: Simon and Scchuster.

Cain, M. (1986). 'Realism, Feminism, Methodology and Law', *International Journal of the Sociology of Law*, 14: 255-67.

——, (1990). 'Towards Transgression : New Directions in Feminist Criminology', *International Journal of the Sociology of Law*, 18 (1) : 1-18.

Carrington, K. and R. Hogg [ed.] (2002). *Critical Criminology : Issues, Debates and Challenges*. Devon: Willan Publishing.

Coomaraswamy, R. (1994). *Violence against Women*, Report of the UN Special Rapporteur, United Nations Economic and Social Commission, Commission of Human Rights, 14 UN. DOC.E/CN.4/1995/42 (1994).

Cook, R. (1995). 'Human Rights and Reproductive Self-Determination', 44, *American University Law Review*.

Cotterrell, R. (1999). *Emile Durkheim : Law in a Moral Domain*. Stanford : Stanford University Press.

Daly, K., and Chesney-Lind (1988). 'Feminism and Criminology', *Justice Quarterly*, 5, 4 :498-538.

Daly, K. (1997). 'Different Ways of Conceptualizing Sex/ Gender in Feminist Theory and their Implications for Criminology', *Theoretical Criminology*, 1, 1 : 25-51.

Dalton, C. (1987). *Berkeley Women's Law Journal* 1, cited in M.D.A. Freedman, Lloyd's Introduction to Jurisprudence, London: Sweet & Maxwell, 1996, p.1028.

Durkheim, E. (1952). *Suicide*. London : Routledge and Kegan Paul.

——, (1964). *The Division of Labour in Society*. New York : Free Press.

Frank, T. M. (1992). 'The Emerging Right to Democratic Governance', *American Journal of International Law*, 86, 46-52.

Garland, D. (2001). *The Culture of Control : Crime and Social Order in Contemporary Society*. Oxford : Oxford University Press.

Garofalo, R. (1885). *Criminology*. Naples, Italy : N.P.

Geertz, C. (1973). *The Interpretation of Culture*, 4-5, New York : Basic Books Inc.

Giddens, A. (1972). *Emile Durkheim : Selected Writings*, Cambridge: Cambridge University Press.

Hanmer, J. & S. Saunders (1984). *Well founded Fear : A Community Study of Violence to Women*, London : Hutchinson.

Heidensohn, F. M. (1968). 'The Deviance of Women : A Critique and an Enquiry'. *British Journal of Sociology*, 19, 160-176.

——, (1996) *Women and Crime,* 2nd Ed., London : Macmillan.

Henry, S. & Milovanovic, D. (1996). *Constitutive Criminology : Beyond Postmodernism.* New Delhi: Sage Publications.

Higgins, T. (1987). 'Democracy and Feminism', 110 *Harvard Law Review,* 1657 at 1676-1685.

Howland, C. W. (1997). *'The Challenges of Religious Fundamentalism to the Liberty and Equality of Rights of Women',* An Analysis under the United Nations Charter, 35, pp. 271-334.

——, (1999). *Religious Fundamentalism and the Human Rights of Women*, London: Macmillan.

Huddard, Y.Y. and Banks T. (1985). *Women, Religion and Social Change.* Albany : State University of New York Press.

Jefferson, T. & Shapland, J. (1994). 'Criminal Justice and the Production of Order and Control : Criminological Research in UK in the 1980s', *British Journal of Criminology*, 34, 3 : 265-90.

Kenny, D. (1936). *Outlines of Criminal Law,* 15th Ed. Cambridge : Cambridge University Press.

Kersten, J. (1996). 'Culture, Masculinity and Violence against Women', *British Journal of Criminology,* 36, 3: 381-95.

Lilly, J. R.; F.T. Cullen; and R. A. Ball (1995). *Criminological Theory : Context and Consequences.* 2nd Edition, New Delhi : Sage Publications.

Mackninnon, C. (1997). *Feminism Unmodified : Discourses on Life and Law,* 1987, Harvard University Press.

——, (1997). 'Rape: On Coercion and Consent', in Kate Conboy, Nadia Medina and Sarah Stanbury (ed.), Writing on the Body: Female Embodiment and Feminist Theory (127-41). New York: Columbia University Press.

Marx, K. Engels, F.C (1970) Selected works. MOSCOW : Progress Publishers.

Maguire, M., R. Morgan & R. Reiner (eds.) [200] *The Oxford Handbook of Criminology*. Oxford : Oxford University Press.

Radzinowicz, L. (1966). *Ideology and Crime : A Study of Crime in its Social and Historical Context*. New York : Columbia University Press.

Schwendinger, H.I. and Schwendinger (1970). "Defenders of Order or Guardians of Human Right," Issues in Criminology 5:123-57

Simon, R. J. (1975). *Women and Crime*, Toronto : Lexington.

Smart, C. (1976). *Women, Crime and Criminology*. London : Routledge and Kegan Paul.

Stanko, E. (1984). *Intimate Intrusions*. London : Routledge and Kegan Paul.

——, (1990). *Everyday Violence*. London: Pandora.

Sutherland, E. H., Cressy, D. R., & Luckenbill, D. F. (1992). *Principles of Criminology* (11 ed.). Dix Hills, NY: General Hall.

Thapan, M. (1997). 'Gender and Embodiment in Everyday life', in M. Thapan (ed.,), *Embodiment: Essays on Gender and Identity*. pp. 1-34, Delhi : Oxford University Press.

Tylor, C. (1987). 'Interpretation and the Science of Man', in *Interpretative Social Science : A Second Look*. Paul Rainbow & W. M. Sullivan (eds) Berkeley : University of California Press.

Taylor, I. (1975). *Critical Criminology*. London: Routledge and Kegan Paul.

——, (1999). *Crime in Context : A Critical Criminology of Market Societies*. Cambridge : Polity Press.

Walby, S. (1989). 'Theorizing Patriarchy', *Sociology*, 23, 2:213-34.

——, (1990). *Theorizing Patriarchy*, Oxford : Blackwell.

——, (1997). *Gender Transformations*, London : Routledge.

W. C. Reckless (1961). The Crime Problem (3rd ed.) New York : Appleton Century Crafts.

Worrall, A. (1990). Offending Women, London : Routledge.

Young, A. (1990). *Femininity in Dissent*. London : Routledge

Young, J. (1986). 'The Future of Criminology', in R. Mathew and J. Young (eds), *Confronting Crime*, London : Sage Publications.

——, (1989). *The Exclusive Society*. London : Sage Publications.

Young, J. & Mathew R. (1992). *Rethinking Criminology : The realist debate*. London : Sage Publications.

Zedner, L. (1991). *Women, Crime and Custody in Victorian England*, Oxford : Oxford University Press.

5

Domestic Violence in Bhopal

Consequences and Coping Mechanisms

Pratima Chaudhary

Introduction

Domestic violence, popularly known as wife battering, is a global phenomena. It occurs among all sections of society irrespective of their birth or worth based background. When wife suffers from mistreatment, injurious action or the abuse of power occurring within the home, it is called wife-battering. There are different roots of wife battering. However, the role of patriarchy, asymmetrical access to and control over the valued resources by the wife in comparison to the husband and provocativeness on the part of wife are some of the necessary conditions in the acceleration of domestic violence. Many scholars have studied different aspects of domestic violence and its impact on victims, children and the concerned families. Important among these are Chaudhary 2001; Coomaraswamy 1995; Dobas and Dobash 1992; Karlekar 1998; Kosambi 1994; Larance 1994; Mahajan 1995; Prasad 1989; Subrahmanian 1995; Tandon 1998 and Thapan 1995. In most of these studies scholars have strongly highlighted the causes and methods of wife battering. The consequences of wife battering and coping mechanisms adopted by the victim themselves and the role of informal organizations in the mitigation of domestic violence only received footnote reference. This Chapter is an attempt to fill this gap.

Methodology

Objectives

More specifically the paper aims to search answer of the following research issues :

- What are the consequences of domestic violence on the concerned women and their children;
- How and to what extent social reputation of the violent families have been affected; and
- What are the coping mechanisms usually followed by the battered women?

Universe/Sample/Procedure

The study was conducted in the city of Bhopal. We could list 150 cases of domestic violence from the local *Mahila Police Station*. These cases were lodged in the police station during the last two years. However, in course of our field work we could trace only 100 battered women. Hence, finally the study was conducted on 100 women. Their complaints are either pending in the police station or it has been forwarded to the court of law. Semi-structured interview schedule and case study were the two techniques employed in this study. Main findings of the study are the following.

Findings and Discussion

Profile

Majority of respondents are between the age group of 15-35 years, they are from all the castes and communities and their natal families are located within the city. Majority of them have lower level of education but 86 per cent of them are from above the poverty line. Majority of them do not own movable or non-movable assets and significant number of them went under debt as violence became a regular feature in their life. Hence, most of the respondents were either from the lower or lower middle class families.

Impact of Violence

Victims

Consequences of domestic violence on the concerned women are of eleven types. However, mental tension, loss of confidence, lack of monetary resource, fear of physical assault on constant basis and loss of prestige was found in the case of large number of respondents in comparison to other consequences like inferiority complex, health loss, fear of divorce/separation, eviction from the house and murder. Many respondents suffered restriction related to their physical mobility, use of household assets, telephone, interaction with neighbour and family friends. Some of the respondents were not allowed even to interact with their children as per their choice. Some of the respondents were even forced to involve in extramarital relations to generate money. For example, N.K. who lodged FIR with the help of *Janwadi Mahila Samiti* separated herself from the husband but her daughter is still with her husband. She lamented, "if he can force his wife to involve in extra-marital relation to earn money, he can also force his daughter to do the same thing. When I think on this issue I get upset. When I was with husband I had lost ego, self-respect and confidence. But now, after separation, I have regained self-respect. Now I am an earning hand".

But there are some women, particularly educated and employed in the government sector who have more tolerance capacity. In spite of violence they do not lose their patience. For example, even during the days of violence the level of self-confidence of S.S, economic condition, and health status did not disintegrate. The only fear which disturbed her was the fear of disorganization of family life.

Table 5.1 : Consequences of Battering on Concerned Women (multiple response)

Sl. No.	*Impact*	*Less*	*More*	*Do Not Know*
1.	Mental tension	000	100	00
2.	Inferiority complex	15	43	42
3.	Lack of confidence	02	69	17
4.	Lack of money	05	67	04
5.	Loss of health	21	43	39
6.	Danger of life	11	49	36
7.	Insult/loss of prestige	05	89	04
8.	Desire to commit suicide	15	09	68
9.	Desire to quit the house	17	08	48
10.	Forced to quit Home	10	22	57
11.	Fear to be Divorced	09	08	83

Children

Impact of domestic violence on children in terms of their health, education, food quality, play and behaviour was assessed. The impact was very negative on health and food quality in the case of more than 50 per cent respondents. Education and entertainment facility was not made available to the children of 40 per cent respondents. In some of the cases (10) behaviour of children drastically changed. They became disobedient, sadist and violent. In response to a question one of the respondents was told by her 12 years old son, "why I should obey you? Even father do not listen to you. I will listen to my grandmother and not you".

Kajari Bai described that, "Children feel frightened and afraid in the tense situation. They apprehend that they may also be beaten any time. As a result, they maintain distance with parents. They are failed to interact with play group children". Her husband abuses the children when they demand money. In fact most part of his income is spent on liquor.

Pravati Bai also supported the feelings of Kajari Bai. Her children have lost confidence and every now and then they

Table 5. 2 : Effect of Battering on Children (multiple response)

Sl. No.	*Nature of effect*	*Health*	*Education*	*Food*	*Play*	*Change in Behaviour*
1.	Good	03	06	04	08	03
2.	Bad	52	40	50	46	10
3.	Undecided	10	04	08	07	06
4.	NR/NA	03	07	02	06	02
Total		**70**	**57**	**64**	**67**	**21**

quarrel and fight among themselves. For him liquor is more important than providing education, etc., to the children.

Kamala Bai (S.C.) lamented that because of neglect of father, her son is most often sick. He fails to attend class/school regularly. She recalled that her husband has extra-marital relations and to please that lady, he spends most part of his earnings on her. He does not allow children to place any demand before him. Since children from neighbourhood know that nobody is behind the boy, therefore, usually they assault the child. The net result of all these negative factors are that the child is physically sick and mentally absent.

Family Reputation

In most of the cases (75 %) domestic violence affected social and economic status of the family in general and the husband in particular, both among relatives and friends. A section of in-laws/husbands disclosed that caste men hesitate to accept daughters of their families as daughter-in-law. In some of the cases daughters of the violent families have adjustment problem as daughter-in-law. In the case of 77 respondents family friends, neighbours, and relatives hesitate to visit to them. Some do not allow their children to play with the children of the violent families. In few of the cases landlords forced their violent tenants to vacate the house.

Coping Mechanisms

Besides constitutional intervention there are different formal organizations working at Bhopal to deal with the problem of domestic violence. These are : Mahila Police Station and its Help Line and Family Counselling Centres, State Human Rights Commission, State Mahila Ayog, Muslim Personnel Court (Kazyat), and All India Women's Conference. In each year they receive dozens of cases. But in most of the cases all these organizations encourage women to adjust with the situation. Women are seldom advised to come out of the violent marital life. Their husbands are first perceived as husband and subsequently as an offender. This perception minimizes the amount of hardness on the part of police and such other agencies against husbands and others. They concentrate more on continuation of marital life in comparison to justice to the concerned women at the cost of breakdown of marital relation.

Here it is needless to mention that before coming to the formal organizations most of the women try at their own to cope up with the hostile situations. They go to police only when they feel that their life is at stake. This is clear from the following illustrations.

(a) Initially respondents did not disclose torture to the unconcerned persons, NGOs or formal organization. 64 per cent narrated the case to the parents. Among the parents 50 reported it only to the mother and remaining 30 to the relatives. Parents were reported about the torture either directly when the respondents visited maternal house or through letter/telephone. They reported their parents to restore normalcy in family life as well as to seek emotional and financial assistance. For example, 89 approached them to seek consolance, 3 for economic support, 42 to advice the husband and 24 to seek help in all related issues. In short, most of the respondents approached the informal sources to convince the husband not to beat the wife.

(b) Majority of the respondents consciously made delay in lodging FIR with the hope that one day situation will improve and tension will disappear. The remaining respondents delayed because of uncertain future after lodging FIR, economic dependence, fear of loss of prestige and lack of self-confidence. Only 4 respondents lodged FIR as soon as they experienced violence. All the 4 are educated and associated with NGOs and their parents strongly helped them in this work.

There are different steps involved in taking decision to lodge case and finally before lodging the FIR. At all these levels a section of women did not seek help from others but majority of them seek help from more than one sources. However, hardly in few cases support came from any formal source. For instance, 48, 12, 10 and 37 respondents received help from their parents, neighbour, women's organization and self-decision respectively. Similarly in order to contact the police or court 43 received help from parents and 7 from neighbours. In short, whether it is registration of case in the court, visiting court or police, in most of the cases respondents either took their own decision or they were helped by their parents. But those who had non-arranged or love marriage initially they did not approach their parents to seek help. They followed all the techniques but informed the parents when they found all these techniques ineffective. For example, S. S., a post-graduate degree holder working in a nationalized bank had non-arranged and inter-caste marriage. She was married to a man with lower social and economic status. The main reason of violence was dowry and inferiority complex on the part of her husband. She adopted following techniques to overcome tension (a) She motivated her parents to manage dowry both in cash and kind as and when the demand was placed; (b) She purchased a separate house with the hope that it will satisfy ego of her husband; (c) But the incidence of October 11, 1994 forced to contact her with mother and narrate the whole story. In response to a question that why did she delayed in seeking help of others including parents, in order to escape violence she said, "I had married him without the consent of my parents. My father is a retired and handicapped man. My brothers were of very young age. Therefore, I decided not to disclose the story of battering. I also kept it secret for several months because the decision to marry with him was a rational decision. It was not at all emotional. I tried my best to satisfy his ego, economic demands and social obligations so that normalcy may be restored. I deliberately tried not to disclose battering with the fear that people may laugh on her. I delayed lodging FIR with the hope of restoration of normalcy in the marital life; and (d) But when hope of normalcy ended she along with her mother (school teacher) approached a voluntary organization (Janwadi Mahila Samiti) for rescue. Finally with the help of the said organization a complaint was lodged in local Mahila Police Station. As a result he was arrested.

Conclusion

It is true that women irrespective of their social and demographic background suffer violence and overall there is negative impact of violence on the concerned women, their children and the family reputation but it is clear that in order to escape violence most of them depend mainly on the informal sources especially parents. Majority of the victims suffer tension in order to save marital life. They report the incident to their parents only when their own efforts become ineffective. They follow dictates of husband with the hope that one day normalcy will return in their life. The amount of suffering is low in case the victim is educated, employed associated with NGOs, have strong support of natal family and in-laws do not cooperate with the husband in the instigation of violence. But in most of the cases reverse is the situation. Since right from the beginning of violence, women approach the informal institutions as a coping mechanism, therefore, it may be suggested that local level NGOs, parents associations, caste organizations, etc; should be encouraged to discourage marital violence. Also, the role of formal organizations should be made available to most of the victims, particularly the poor women. In many cases dowry is the main root of violence. Hence, it is suggested that Dowry Prohibition Act should be implemented honestly. Organization of awareness camp on regular basis can also be an effective intervention in this direction. Empowerment of women along with inculcation of social values in both men and women can also play significant role in this direction.

References

Chaudhary, P. (2001) : *Battered Women : A Study of Domestic Violence,* Bhopal, Porvasha Prakashan.

Coomaraswamy, R. *(1995) : Violence Against Women,* New Delhi, Indian Association of Women's Studies, pp. 4-7.

Dobas, R. E and R. P. Dobash (1992): *Women, Violence and Social Change,* London Routledge.

Karlekar, M. (1998) : "Domestic Violence", *EPW,* July 4-10, pp. 17-47.

Kosambi (1994) : Women's Oppression in the *Public Gaze, Bombay, Centre* for Women's Studies, SNDT University, pp. 4-14.

Larance, L. (1994) : *Marital Violence in Canada,* Bombay, SNDT University, pp. 89-91.

Mahajan, A. (1995) : *Family Violence and Abuse in India,* New Delhi : Madhurma, pp. 29-59.

Prasad, M. B. (1989) : "Violence Against Women : A Review of Literature," (ed) Niroj Sinha, *Women and Violence,* New Delhi, Vikas Publications.

Subrahmanian, R. (1995) : "Combating Violence Against Women," *The Administrator,* Vol. XI, September, pp. 45-59.

Tandon, L.S. (1998) : "Violence and Tension in the Family," *Social Change,* September, pp. 14-44.

Thapan, M. (1995) : "Images of the Body and Sexuality in Women's Narratives and Oppression in the Home", *EPW,* 28th October, 1995.

6

Girl Child on the Verge of Extinction

Battles begin in Womb

Namrata Sharma

She was reassured about her future and her small dreams. For she was just overwhelmed by the warmth provided with by her mother. The latter held her in her womb. But, the mind held something else. The mother threw a keen glance at a roadside advertisement. The graffiti read :

"Ladaka hi hogaa. Sheeghra milein. Sau per cent guarantee. Card saath laye. (Birth of baby boy is assured. See us soon. Guarantee card with 100 per cent assurance provided)." It was placed by one of the thousands of professionals selling death for the 'selected sex'. A few days later, she saw herself been aborted and drained out. She died before she could be born. And the dreams died first— B.Nathesan.

Introduction

Violence against women is present in every country, cutting across boundaries of culture, class, education, income, ethnicity and age. There are 50 million fewer women in South Asia today than there should be — girl babies are killed before birth through sex-selective abortions, or die prematurely through violence and neglect. Female foeticide is one extreme manifestation of violence against women. Millions more girls and women face discrimination — they have less to eat than boys and men, are denied an education, are forced into dowry marriages, have little or no access to health services, and suffer violence. It is agonizing to know that the gender bias and deep-rooted prejudice and discrimination against girl child, which have been there down the centuries, are now found to begin in the womb itself. The girl child in the womb faces the peril of pre-birth elimination, i.e., female foeticide. Female foetuses are selectively aborted after pre-natal sex determination, thus avoiding the birth of girls. In India where female infanticide has existed for centuries, now female foeticide has joined the fray and is increasing each day .Doctors in India believes 2 million foetuses are killed every year through abortion, simply because they are female, even though it is an illegal practice. And with the increasing availability of sex determination tests it is impossible to keep track of such cases.

The girl children in India have been the most vulnerable for centuries and, are even today, vulnerable to the insults of deprivation as well as discrimination. In particular, peculiar to South Asia, and certainly to India, tradition, values and customs encrusted over time have resulted in the insatiable desire for sons, with families having totally marginalized the joy and pleasure in giving birth to a baby girl. In South Asia, we have inherited the cultural legacy of strong son-preference among all communities, religious groups and citizens of varied socio-economic backgrounds. The girl child has traditionally been considered inferior and a liability.

In India, there is a deep-rooted ancient concept of having a son to carry on with the name and tradition of the family. Right from childhood, girls are made to accept the norms of patriarchal and male dominated society. Even our religion have been prejudiced towards women. According to Manu (2000 BC-2000 AD), a woman has to be reborn as a man to attain *moksha* (redemption). A man cannot attain *moksha* unless he has a son to light his pyre. A male offspring alone guarantees *moksha*. And he attains eternity through a grand-son. In the *Manusmriti*, it is provided that woman in her childhood must remain under the custody of her father, in youth she must remain under the custody of her husband and when widowed she must remain under the custody of her sons. She must never be independent whether minor or young or old. Manu held the male as the enjoyer and female as a 'thing' to be enjoyed. The bride is given to the bridegroom with a solemn declaration that the former, like dining leaf, not to be used by someone else, is not to be enjoyed by any person other than the latter. Such gender bias leads to incidences such as female infanticide and female foeticide.

However, the practice *of* foeticide, in which an unborn baby is aborted or killed at birth simply because it is not a boy, is increasingly spreading from India's poor and rural classes to affluent urban families. If the female foetus is lucky enough to survive till her birth then she faced the peril of elimination in infancy by female infanticide. (Kolloor, 1990) defined it as, "Killing of an entirely dependent girl child under one year of age by mother, parents or others in whose care she is entrusted". Historically, female infanticide has been in existence since long. Girl infants have been known to be killed by rubbing poison on the mother's breast, by feeding infants with milk of errukam flower or oleander berries, by using sap of calotropis plant, paddy grains, giving sleeping tablets or by simply burying the girl infants alive.

Female infanticide was common among certain castes and tribes such as Rajputs, Jats, Gujars, Ahirs and Sikhs. It was a custom widely accepted among these warrior tribes, where sons were needed to defend the honour and more important, the territories of the tribe. In Punjab, because of martial and agricultural traditions, there has always been a demand for sons to go into battle or who would plough fields during peace time.

Today, India tops the list as far as illegal abortions and female infanticide are concerned. Of the 15 million illegal abortions carried out in the world in 1997, India accounted for four million, 90 per cent of which were intended to eliminate the girl child. Elimination of the female foetus is a case of discrimination and elimination on the basis of gender and cannot be treated as a tool for family planning. Nor can it be deemed as a matter of personal preference or discretion. A sex-selected abortion is legally punishable offence. For it is the murder of a 'girl child' — yet to take birth—without bringing to effect Act 302 of the Indian Penal Code.

Saheli, a Delhi based NGO, has reported that between 1978-82, nearly 78,000 female foetuses were aborted after sex determination tests in the country. Between 1986-87, 30,000 to 50,000 female foetuses had been aborted. Between 1982-92, the number of sex determination clinics multiplied manifold and nearly 13,000 sex determination tests were estimated to have been done in seven Delhi clinics themselves (Gurung).

Social pressures in India, and the presence of low cost technologies like ultrasound, have led to sex-based abortion of female foetuses, and an increasingly smaller percentage of girls born each year. It is not only the poor, but even the middle classes and the rich in India that are biased against the girl child and women. The problem is mainly in the region where the status of women is still relatively low and demand for sons high.

Selection of the sex of the foetus is a combination of personal choices, family issues, social, ethical, medical and even legal reasons. Girls are considered as second class citizens as they provided no social security to parents in old age. Another key reason for foeticide has been the system of dowry, prevalent in rural as well as now increasingly in urban India. Girls took dowry from their parents while sons brought huge amount of dowry for their parents.

Foeticide is a far bigger social evil than dowry. The

deterioration of women's status and the emergence of female foeticide is not a unique sociological phenomenon confined to a particular State. The trend is all over the country.

Gender Preferences

According to a recent report by the United Nations Children's Fund (UNICEF) up to 50 million girls and women are missing from India's population as a result of systematic gender discrimination in India.

In India, there are less than 93 women for every 100 men in the population. India has traditionally been a male dominated society. There is a strong son preference in most parts of India, and girls tend to be discriminated against by their families. The accepted reason for such a disparity is the practice of female infanticide in India, prompted by the existence of a dowry system which requires the family to pay out a great deal of money when a female child is married which is a major drain on household resources (Menski, 1998). For a poor family, the birth of a girl child can signal the beginning of financial ruin and extreme hardship. Girls are often denied the right to education, since expense on her education is not considered to be an investment of higher returns. According to Janice Raymond (1994, p. 24) girls are breastfed for a shorter period of time, which denies their right to adequate health and nutrition. They are taken to fewer medical consultations and often very late or not at all to the hospitals (Dreze and Sen 1995).Girls are also not immunized, failure of which leads to poor health and sickness.

In an age when females have made progress in almost every field, there are people who still accord a lower status to women. In some of our Indian societies, while a childless woman is perceived as incomplete, one who has given birth to daughters is partially complete. Only the one who has produced a son enjoys a status of all sorts (Sharma, 2005).

The Sex Ratio is given in Chart 6.1 from 1901 to 2001 and also the Year-Sex Ratio (Females per 1,000 males)

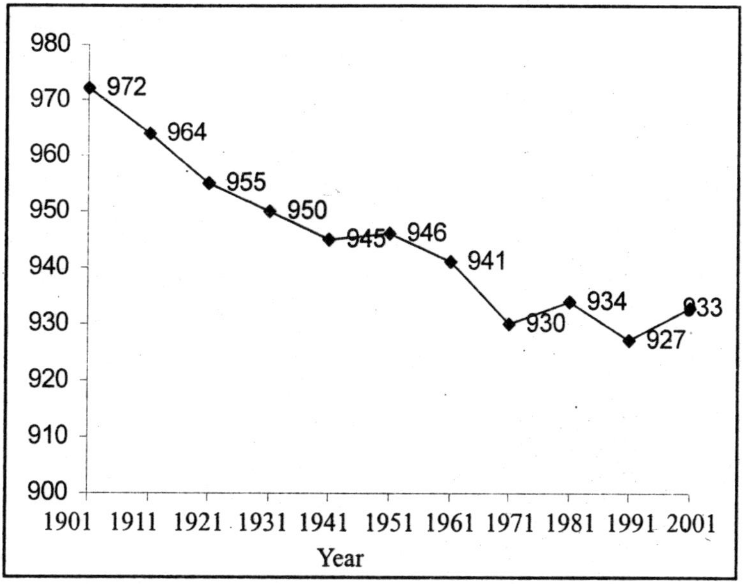

Chart 6.1 : Sex Ratio in India over the Years

Source : Census of India.

India is one of the few countries in the world where males outnumber females. The sex ratio of Indian population has shown a secular declining trend except some marginal increases in the censuses of 1951, 1981 and 2001.The net deficit of females, which was 3.2 million in 1901 has now widened to over 35 million in 2001. The sex ratio in 2001 was 933, six points higher than the sex ratio of 927 recorded in 1991. Miller in her study "The endangered Sex" (1981) emphasized the socio-.cultural discrimination against female children as the main reason for female mortality.

Prevalence and spread of female Foeticide

In India, the practice of sex-selective abortion or female foeticide is only the latest manifestation of a long history of gender bias, evident in the historically low and declining population ratio of women to men.

Female foeticide is reported in 27 of India's 32 States, and the impact on the sex ratio among young children is alarming. The regional disparities also appear to have increased; the northern States generally exhibit a worsening trend in male-female ratio as compared to southern States. The sex ratio imbalances are more severe in north-western region, which stretching from Uttranchal in the north runs up to Maharashtra in the west across Himachal Pradesh, Punjab, Chandigarh, Haryana, Delhi, Rajasthan and Gujarat. The declining numbers are most pronounced in the economically advanced States of Punjab and Gujarat. NFHS survey demonstrated that ultrasound and amniocentesis are often used for sex determination and sex selective abortions of female foetuses have been rampant in many States of India, particularly in Punjab, Haryana and Gujarat.

This practice of foeticide is most common among India's elite, who can afford multiple trips to an ultrasound clinic, and the hushed-up abortion of an unwanted girl. In the prosperous farming district of Kurukshetra, for instance, there are only 770 girl babies for every 1,000 boys. In the high-rent south-west neighbourhood of New Delhi, the number of girl babies is 845 per 1,000 boys.

The problem of sex ratio is worst in the north-western States, where the ratio is less than 900 girls for every 1,000 boys. In Punjab it is estimated that one in five girl children is missing due to selective abortions. In Punjab there are only 874 females per 1,000 males.

The situation in Haryana, Gujarat and Maharashtra is also similar — the females are 861, 921 and 922 respectively per 1,000 males. Kerala is the only State where females are 1,058 per 1,000 males.

Index of Son Preference for Major States, 1990 Index of Son Preference =100 (EC)

Table showing the ranks of various states along the index of son preference

States	*Index of Son Preference*	*Rank*
Andhra Pradesh	13.8	11
Bihar	24.5	4
Gujarat	23	6
Haryana	14.3	10
Karnataka	20	8
Kerala	11.7	12
Madhya Pradesh	27.1	2
Maharashtra	18	9
Orissa	23.4	5
Punjab	20.3	7
Rajasthan	25	3
Tamil Nadu	9.2	13
Uttar Pradesh	21.6	1
West Bengal	14.3	10
All India	20	

Source : Decline in juvenile sex ratio : Index of son preference for major states in India 1990.

Decline in juvenile sex ratio (DSR) in the most distressing factor reflecting premium accorded to girl child in our country.

Decline in juvenile sex ratio is seen as index of son preference $= 100\left(\frac{E}{C}\right)$

Where, E =the excess number of sons over daughters considered ideal.
C=ideal family size

The BIMARU States (Bihar, Madhya Pradesh, Rajasthan, Uttar Pradesh) are at the top of the rank for son preference in 1990. Orissa is 5th in rank. Kerala is ranked 12th in the index of son-preference.

2 Education and Foeticide

The practice of foeticide is common among all religious groups — Hindus, Sikhs, Jains, Muslims, and Christians — but appears to be most common among educated women. Modern techniques such as amniocentesis and ultrasound tests have given women greater power to detect the sex of their babies in time to abort. Illegal abortion, particularly of female foetuses, either self-inflicted or performed by unskilled birth attendants, under poor sanitary conditions has led to increased maternal mortality, particularly in South and South-East Asia. Sex discrimination was always considered to be the result of lack of education. But education it seems does not play a role in curbing social evils like female foeticide. In fact more and more educated mothers in several regions are using their education to access modern technology to kill their unborn daughters. According to the interpretations of the recently released fertility series data of Census 2001, the more educated the mother, the greater the chance that she will resort to female foeticide. The census statistics (Chart-6.2) reveal a wide gap in the rural and urban area. In 2001 the sex ratio in rural area was 946 as compared to 900 in urban areas.

This is substantiated by the fact that the decline in girl sex ratio is steep in the urban centres as compared to the rural areas. The literacy growth is higher in the urban centres than in the rural areas. The trend is clearly suggestive of the growing need to eliminate the girl child in order to emerge economically stronger. Literacy and rising incomes only make it easy for couples to get rid of the girl child. Access to latest technology, which obviously comes at a high price, is responsible for the growing foeticide. In Punjab, the girl-boy ratio is 845 : 1000 where the mother is illiterate but only 745 : 1000 where the mother is literate.

Among the educated families, adoption of small family norms means a minimum one son in the family. They can do without daughters. The propertied classes do not desire daughters because after marriage of the daughter, the son-in-law may demand a share in the property. The propertyless class disposes of daughters to avoid dowry harassment. But they do not mind accepting dowry for their sons. The birth of a son is perceived, as an opportunity for upward mobility while the birth of a daughter is believed to result in downward economic mobility.

Sex Ratio of Population by Religion/SC/ST

Sex ratios are declining more in the case of the Hindus, including Scheduled Castes, than in the case of other communities. The worst thing is that this evil has percolated down to among the tribes and other Scheduled Castes that were hitherto unknown to be practicing it. Due to the zooming dowry demands and marriage expenses according to respective classes, the economically lower and middle classes have been reported to be in practice of foeticide and infanticide.

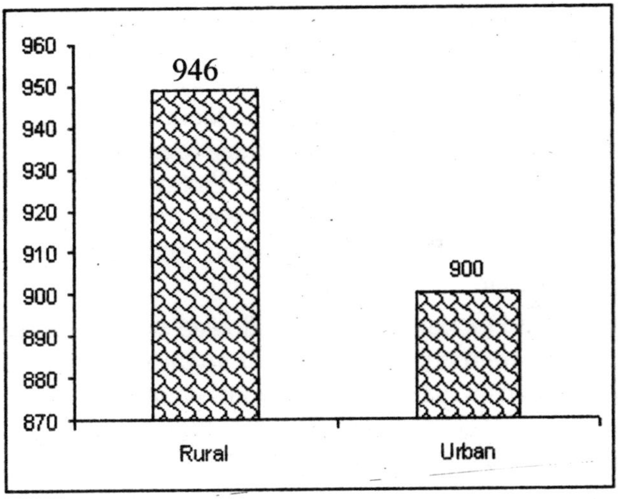

Chart 6.2 : Sex Ratio in Rural and Urban Areas, 2001

Sikhs, who represent one of the most progressive communities in the country, show a very adverse sex ratio, compared to other communities. Satish Agnihotri, an expert on the sex ratio, calls the land rich States of Haryana, Punjab and Uttar Pradesh the "Bermuda Triangle," where girls go missing.

Scenario of Female Foeticide in Madhya Pradesh

Problem of female foeticide and female infanticide are high in Madhya Pradesh especially in upper caste communities. In Madhya Pradesh, the Gurjar, the Yadav (Ahir) and the Rajput communities have particularly low child sex ratios. Among these communities, female infanticide is widely practiced even now.

In Gwalior division especially Bhaduria and Tonwar Rajputs have very low figures (637 and 623 per 1000 males respectively). The point to notice here is that the present proportion of females at the age of 0-6 in the case of these two communities is the lowest as compared to any other caste of significance.

The ravines of Bhind and Morena have long been associated with tales of female infanticide, today with increasing number of ultrasound clinics which provide safe heaven for illegal foetal sex determination these silent landmarks stand witness to the growing practice of female foeticide. The region chiefly inhabited by the Gurjars, Yadavs and Rajputs, encompasses the Chambal belt that was once notorious for dacoits. Here, feudal practices dominate and display of guns is a sign of valour.

Rajputs and Gurjars normally followed the rule of hypergamy and the marriage of a daughter involved a huge dowry and other expenses, which many Rajputs were unable to meet. To save themselves from dishonour, they destroyed their daughters. It seems that some of these traditions or practical difficulties continue to force people to destroy their daughters. The Rajputs in Bhind district are an extremely male dominated lot with a very strong son preference. According to the doctor, when a male child is born, the woman is kept in the hospital for two to three days, but when a girl child is born the villagers take the woman home immediately, even at odd hours, so that the child can be put to rest by feeding her tobacco. The practice of female foeticide and infanticide is prevalent only in certain communities of Madhya Pradesh and the factors responsible and generally reported are high costs of dowry and prevailing custom of hypergamy which hurts the pride of Rajputs and leads to imbalance in child sex ratio.

Conclusion

The desire to accumulate wealth has become an increasingly important factor in son preference in recent years. As a result of the desire among the growing middle class for upward mobility son preference is strong. There is a dire need to sensitize people against the practice of female foeticide.

The spread of consumerism and the associated increase in the cost of dowry and marriage, plus the desire to maintain landholdings within a family all have contributed to an environment that is extremely hostile to women and girl children, even among the educated middle and upper classes. Enforcing a law is not enough but there is a need to change the mindset of the people that empowers women and improves upon her overall status in the society.

References

Annual Report on implementation of the *Pre-conception and Pre-Natal Diagnostic Techniques (Prohibition of Sex Selection) Act*, 2005.

Ashish Bose, *Demographic Diversity of India, 1991 Census, D K Publishers,* New Delhi, July,1991.

B.Nathesan, Silent Scream (Source website).

Dreze, Jean and Amartya Sen. *1995*. India: *Economic development and social opportunity*. Delhi: Oxford University Press.

Gurung, Madhu, *Female Foeticide*, Chaitanya The Policy Consultancy, Sept.10, 2005.

IIPS (1995). *National Family Health Survey 1992-1993*, India., Bombay: International Institute for Population Sciences. IIPS and ORC Macro (2001). *National Family Health Survey (NFHS-2) - India 1998-99*, Mumbai : International Institute for Population Sciences.

Kollor, T. M. (1990) "Female Infanticide: A Psychological Analysis". *Grass Roots Action, Special issue on Girl Child,* April 3, p.3.

Menski, Werner (ed.) (1998). South Asians and the Dowry Problem, Trentham Books, London.

Miller, B.D. (1981). *The Endangered Sex*, Cornell University Press, Ithaca, New York.

Premi, M.K. and Saraswathi Raju (1998). "Born to Die: Female Infanticide in Madhya Pradesh," *Economic and Political Weekly*, Vol. 32, No.17.

Rajan S.I., U.S. Mishra and T.K. Vimla (1996) Choosing a Permanent Contraceptives : Does Son Preference Matter? Economic and Political Weekly, July, p. 20, 1980.

Raymond, J. G. (1994). In *Women As Wombs,* Spinifex, Melbourne, Registrar General and Census Commissioner, India, 2001.

Sen, A. (1990). More than 100 Million Women are Missing, New York Review of Books,20. Dec., pp. 61-66

Sharma, Chentan and Divya Jain, *Technology and its Impact on Female Foeticide*, Digital Communities, May 18, 2005.

Source : SAHELI, A Delhi based NGO UNICEF.

7
Women in the Business of Selling Sex
A Socio-Gendered Perspective

Meghna Sanyal

The study of women embroiled within the experiences of sex trade has become quite significant; questioning the basic survival in their livelihood process. The wenches who have either been deserted by their husbands or those who just managed to escape the tyranny of masculine forces within the domestic space, the unskilled female labour force situated within the unorganised sector of the economy are eventually lured to the beguiling gateway of sex trade. The entire process thus becomes an aviary which has got just one way entry with no exits whatsoever.

A poor woman after the death of her husband might not find a shelter, safe and adequate so to speak, nor could she depend on her hereditary cottage industries, if any. It is conjecturable that in such a condition, she, finding life intolerable fell an easy prey to the profession of sex trade. Even the upper caste women could hardly escape from the clutches of this profession. (Joarder, 1985). It is here that I begin my discussion on the identification of the issue on sex trade as a social problem and how this affects the social conditioning of the images of women in general.

The economic and social insecurity, often makes, those women who have been ceded by their husbands, a volatile entity, as a result of which they are perpetually drawn into the viscious web of global sex trade. The dearth of jobs in the third world countries tempts the women to take up the overseas pursuits which are necessarily the sex-trade occupation and in the process of selling sexual labour; the sex worker often loses their self-respect. In India, the panorama holds a different picture. In most of the poor households, the married man migrates to different cities and more often to different countries for their livelihood, abandoning their young wife and children back at home. These poverty driven unskilled labourers in seeking to get in different overseas occupation gradually estrange themselves from the near ones mortifying the relationships at all levels. The wives and children who are left back at home are, therefore, troubled at large extent; in despair, they begin to seek jobs as domestic helpers and other such unskilled works and in the process the young maidens fall prey in the hands of the traffickers who promise them a job and secretly turn them as sex slaves. Trafficked victims endure physical, psychological and sexual abuse. Their movement is severely restricted and they have virtually no privacy. Their health and safety are constantly at risk, and unknown members die every year from abuse, neglect, murder and suicide.

One of the arguments in support of sexual slavery, advanced by the American supporters of the institution, was that the Southern whites, being all freed from servile duties, could maintain the most democratic and refined relations among themselves; in the same way, a caste of "shameless women" allows the "honest woman" to be treated with the most chivalrous respect. The prostitute is a scapegoat; man vents his turpitude upon her, and he rejects her. Whether she is put legally under police supervision or works illegally in secret, she is in any case treated as a pariah (Beauvoir, 1989).

In support of the literatures that I have consulted while writing this chapter will be narrated in this section. The pressure of the very survival of the women hailing from the rural background drags them to the apparent decoying profession which lures them in the beginning but gradually turns them peevish. This drudgery, involving a soporific yet ruinous lifestyle, never invigorates their mind and ceaselessly hauls them into more and more virulence. The following literature narrates an account of a female labour migration from the third world nations to that of the wealthy counterparts. In *Global Women: Nannies, Maids and Sex Workers in the New Economy*, ed., *Barbara Ehrenreich and Arlie Hochschild*, the authors narrate the story of Josephine, a Sri Lankan lady, a nanny by profession, who has migrated to the wealthier nation in search of jobs. In it, the author says, "The lifestyles of the First World are made possible by a global transfer of the services associated with a wife's traditional role— child care, home-making, and sex—from poor countries to the rich. Similarly, women who migrate from country to country to work as maids bring not only their muscle power but an attentiveness to detail and to the human relationships in the household that might otherwise have been invested in their own families. Sex workers offer the stimulation of sexual and romantic love, or at least transient sexual companionship. It is as if the wealthy parts of the world are running short on precious emotional and sexual resources and have to turn to poorer regions for fresh supplies. The author here specks the crisis of the female labour migration vehemently.

In making the issue of sex-trade such obvious is closely connected with the question of sexuality. India has been facing the *devadasi* system from the dawn of its civilisation and it is only towards the late nineteenth century that the disposition of the profession itself is on the move. *Bahni, Sex trade with Religious Sanction: The Devadasi Problem, Venkatasani, Jogini and the Basavi Cult, Joint Women's Project, 1989.* This study covers Karnataka and Maharashtra. It points out that girls are initiated from the lower castes, such as the *Holeyar* and the *Madars*; there is a nexus between untouchability and particular forms of sex trade, such as *basavi*, *venkatasani* and *jogini*. This is an informative piece of research. The geographical spread and causes (mostly poverty and the low status of women) of these practices are well mapped. Social prejudices and superstitions are also specified. So, here we find that both poverty and the institution of caste affecting the lives of women incessantly.

The illustrated analysis of the markets of flesh trade, centres of transit, supply and demand places a vivid explanation on the issue of sexual exploitation of women and children in today's society. The book on *Trafficking in Women and Children in India: Sexual Exploitation and Sale* by Rozario *et al.* projects the statistics of the intra– and inter State flesh trade transits and recommends a humanitarian and community approach towards eradication of Sex trade in India. Some of the areas where Trafficking in women and children is carried out :

Rae Bareli, Uttar Pradesh————————Morena, Madhya Pradesh
Patna and West Bengal————————Varanasi, Uttar Pradesh
Rajasthan————————Uttar Pradesh
Howrah, West Bengal————————Shahjanpur
Bangladesh————Uttar Pradesh————Delhi
(*Source:* Rozario, 1988)

The facts mentioned above reveals the facts that there are certain junctions where the major trafficking circuit operates. And the facts also provides us the information as there are certain exit points of the trafficked girls and the areas are found near waterbodies. The statistics shows from which State the maximum trafficking takes place and how the network functions in each of the different places; and persons responsible for the Sexual Exploitation of Women and Children in India.

The Table 7.1 shows that the highest number of persons responsible for the sexual exploitation of women and children is their own "kith and kin". This comprises of 353 persons, representing 33 per cent of the sample. These are loved persons on whom the women and children depended and had a trust in course of their survival and sustenance. A more

Table 7.1 : Number and Percentage of Persons Responsible for Trafficking of Women

Sl. No.	*Persons Responsible*	*Frequency*	*Percentage*
1.	Kith and Kin	353	33
2.	Friends and Acquaintances	66	6
3.	Strangers and Benefactors	115	10
4.	Persons involved in flesh-trade	208	19
5.	Persons at the service of society	66	6
6.	Information not available/not applicable	292	26
	Total	1100	100

Source: Rozario, 1988, Page 117.

specific break up of this group of persons under Kith and Kin shows they are: aunt (1); brother (2); brother-in-law (6); brother and purchaser (1); elders i.e., parents and guardians (213); elder sister (1); father (19); in-laws (1); husband (4); grandmother (3); maternal uncle (1); sisters (2); parents (19); stepmother (1); uncle (2); mother (27). One often presumes that women and children are sexually exploited only through an organised network of gangs, etc., at distant places. It is surprising to see how the close and near persons who sexually exploit our women and children in India.

Bombay's red light area is a sensuous and sinister underworld. There are over 50,000 *rundies*, 20,000 *bhadwas, years, dadas and mafias*. Over 6,000 *gharwalis, goons, thugs* and other *goondas* involved in violence and narcotics, illicit contraband gambling and 15,000 male sex workers or hijras with an equal number of their agents with expert knowledge and sexual perversion. They all are in their business openly without fear. It is world dominated by sex, violence, drugs and diseases. (Rozario,1988). Women and children, sexually exploited and sold, consider the attitudes and behaviour of society towards them as an ultimate betrayal of love and rejection. Being born a woman.in the Indian society places her with a low status in the social hierarchy and a fact of becoming a *prostitute* further lower the status. She is treated as a non-human and accepted more as a commodity to satisfy men's sexual needs and desires. The condition of women and children is to endure something beyond our comprehension. (Rozario, 1988)

A Glance to the Review of the Organisation of Sex Trade from Ancient to the Modern Era

To spoor the institution of sex trade in pre-industrial era, I have drawn references from the various literary texts which were drafted at the dawn of Indian civilization. The religious mystical roles in both East and West have a erotic component. Sex as a worshipful expressive communication with a supra individual force is illustrated by the activities of temple sex workers in Babylon. In Cyprus and Corinth, the act took place in a temple and was a religious ritual. Sacred sex workers were among aphrodites, priestesses. Unimpeded by any knowledge of the woman as an individual, the male worshipper was able, through her body to touch the very essence of sexuality— the divine essence. Adultery has been overwhelming fact of life, a timeless pastime of the peasantry and the nobility alike. Sexual communism was the order of the day in the primitive communities. A male partner was the husband of all and, therefore, of none. Consequently, sex trade was not treated as a problem during those times. The practice of sex trade was an expression of hospitality. Herodotus, the ancient historian, records that even kings used to offer their daughters to the guests. In Hydia, girls used to earn their dowry through sex trade which had religious sanction. (Raghuramaiah, 1991)

In Indian Mythology, we find the characters embedded under the connotation of *apsaras* as god's female dancers, clever in dancing and singing. They are described as uncommonly beautiful with lotus eyes, slender waists and swelling hips. By ravishing postures, roguish and sweet conversations they robbed the spectator of thought and intellect. They deck heroes with wreathes and precious stones. The names of the *apsaras* that we hear of are Urvashi, Rambha, Sahajanya, Menaka, Tilottama and Ghritachi. They were used to entertain the guests in the court of *Indra*, the king of all gods in Hindu mythology. Besides, being a means of amusement they were often sent to disrupt the penance of the other sages, for Indra lived in perpetual fear that his position would be usurped by some sage with the help of ascetic merit. Sometimes, the nymph would succeed in seducing the sage and distracting them from meditation while at other times, they would merely incur the wrath of the sage.(Fausboll, 1981)

So, this shows that even in the Indian mythology the existence of the characters of the different kinds of charmers were still present and they were merely used as eternal sexual objects. There were another group of entertainers in Indra's court and they were called *gandharvas*. They were called musicians of heaven. They played on *veena* (an Indian musical instrument) and sing songs in a melodious tune. In India, the Vedas, the earliest of the known Indian literature, abound in references to sex trade as an organised and established institution.The two great epics of the Indian literature, the *Ramayana* and the *Mahabharata* unveil the institution of sex trade during the reign of Pandavas and Kauravas. They were important part of the court and both the dynasties possessed *harems* of aristocracy in Brahmanic India as having concubines were common during that era. *Kautilya's Arthasastra* depicts certain rules for sex workers and their activities and provides a vivid account of how sex workers should behave and how their lives are ordered. A code of conduct was prescribed, for people seeking their favour and for them, which included certain definite prerogatives, rights and duties. The sanctified sex trade of the third century is mentioned in the Sanskrit works of Mahakavi Kalidas. Religious sex trade, constituted by a class of girls, who had been offered by the parents to the service of gods and their religion, were attached to the famous temples of Mahakala of Ujjain and the system of holy sex workers became common. (Fausboll, 1981)

Indian history has given a mixed deal to the prostitute. From the earliest literature it is evident that sex trade was a very prevalent practice. Rig Veda mentions both sex trade and illegitimate children. Atharva Veda has many descriptive passages of vagabond priests and their female companions who were sacred sex workers. There was a class of specialists, the vratyas, particularly connected with the region of Magadha. They were outside the regular system of vedic religion. They travelled from place to place in a bullock cart with an apprentice and with a woman who appears to have been used for ritual sex trade. Jataka tales also give evidences how sex workers were not only tolerated but were also respected by the public. They were accomplished women. The fees paid to some of them were exceedingly high. It is in the Buddhist legends that we read of Ambalpata, the famous courtesan of Vaishali. Among those who joined the profession was a person of no less status than Princess Salawati. Vatsyayan devoted an entire part of his celebrated Hindu ritual of love Kama Sutra to courtesans and sex workers. He begins with the matter of fact, the statement that men provide pleasure and a means of earning a livelihood (Raghuramaiah, 1991). So, when men is doing a duty to society it is always expected that a woman should behave as if she loved him, because men prefer women who are devoted and attentive to them. His ten commandments for the women were :

1. *Dress well;*
2. *Make friends with well connected people;*
3. *Practice the trade among the pleasure loving, the rich and the vain glorious and powerful;*
4. *Be choosy, stick to men with excellent qualities;*
5. *When living with a man be faithful;*

6. *Be attentive to his accounts of his good works and never neglect to remind his generous actions;*
7. Make *love to him the way he likes it;*
8. *When on the path of merciless ruin Kama overtakes Artha, so when you find the man is ruined take another rich one for your client and discard the former;*
9. *If a courtesan can each day earn a lot of money because she has a large clientele she should not attach herself to one man;* and
10. *When you have too much money donate towards the construction of temples, rituals and religious ceremonies.*

—Raghuramaiah, 1991, p. 40

The picture that is depicted by Vatsyayan about a prostitute reveals that of a social woman eager to join gatherings of the nobility. Kautilya gave an account of the utility of the sex workers to the public exchequer. They could be used as spy. His line of thinking has its impact for centuries. In the 15th century, Vijay Nagar sex workers were kept in state controlled brothels, the revenue of which went to upkeep of the sex workers. Abdul Razzak, a Turkish Ambassador, has left a lively record of such brothels. During the Mughal Age, Akbar tried to bring some sort of control and supervision on the sex workers. During the reign of Shahjahan lover, dancers and public women enjoyed great liberty and were found in great numbers in cities. During the reign of Aurangzeb, sex trade went underground.

Trafficking in women and sexual abuse prevailed in pre-industrial as well as in feudal era as agriculture was the major source of production then, and women were excluded from the public sphere. Women's status were further reduced to a mere sexual objects and they were considered to be the property of their husbands. Under such conditions, women were governed by marital relations of power through exploitation of their unpaid labour in home, their fecundity and sexuality.

They were, therefore, privatised in the hands of patriarchal power at home as a result of which their labour outside homes was confined within the informal economic sector. Sexual subordination and economic dependency resulting from women's status as the property of their husbands is marital feudalism. In feudalism, men may sexually exploit their wives, take concubines and buy sex workers with impunity as the privilege of male domination that serves their promiscuity. By contrast, as women are sexual properties of men, any sexual act outside their marriage, including rape and forced sex trade, is usually considered infidelity and victims are severely punished. Again, in private patriarchal sector, women and girls are supplied to brothels through brutal trafficking and forced sex trade. (Kevin, 2005). Military sex trade in war and in many areas where there is a massive military presence provided for soldiers for rest and recreation. Therefore, military sex trade proliferates in the areas where women are vulnerable from war, and in the patriarchal traditionalism of the society where war is waged, makes women and girls accessible to be prostituted as sex commodities for foreign soldiers usually aggressors or occupiers.

Aftermath the Industrial Revolution, the rise of patriarchal supremacy was considerably noted. Sexual Exploitation is, therefore, differentially shaped according to the economic development of each region, which determines the fact of how sex is socially constructed and deployed to subordinate women. While each of the stages of sexual exploitation are found in any historical period or in any stage of a country's economic development, they also constitute progression along with economic development and prosperity. Sex trade was organised by certain cults as a service to the goddess of love. The advent of slave women and their abundant supply debased sex trade. The lords wanted beautiful slaves who were reduced to the pleasure machines to be used as adlibs. As the dark age proceeded, the inhumanity attributed towards women in general multiplied. The severe punishments were sometimes awarded to the sex workers where a whore received three hundred strokes with a whip, and each of the members of the family used to receive hundred each. During the middle ages, the states of Western Europe tolerated sex trade but certain regulations were imparted. First, brothel was considered to be a necessary social service in the city life because it was believed that sex workers could satisfy the lecherous impulse so that daughters of the decent folk would be saved. Second, aim of medieval regulation was to prevent the brothel from becoming a centre of disorder. Third, sex trade was regulated so as to serve the fiscal purpose. (Raghuramaiah, 1991)

Sex industrialization accompanies economic development. With Industrialization and the development of public economic sector, large number of women leave their private households in search of jobs in the public economy, usually in urban areas as industrializing economies shifts from domestic to export oriented production.

Persistent Flesh Trade in the Sub-Continent in the Present Era

The flesh trade has become quite popular globally and has its varied forms. In India, there are inter-State and intra-State flesh trade triangles which act as the transit centres. The data shows that the inter-State transit centres are usually located near the boundary of the States. Therefore, this affords easy transference of women and children from one State to another with the necessary natural protection. These areas are mostly isolated from the heart of the city and, therefore, brings immense sufferings to the victims, who are mostly children and minor, and they find a strange environment with a different language and are unable to find their way back to home. Intra-state flesh markets are within the reach of local procurers and they function as supply centres as well. These triangles facilitate internal flesh trade. Uttar Pradesh in the north and Tamil Nadu in the south function as demand, supply and transit centres. Varanasi on the banks of the river Ganges in Uttar Pradesh and Madurai with its Meenakshiammam Temple in Tamil Nadu are both religious and tourist centres in India. The area is usually over-crowded in festive seasons and the well connected transportation system makes it an easy pitch for the flesh traders. (Rozario, 1988). In recent years the Indian sub-continent has emerged as a hotspot in the South Asian region for trafficking in persons. It is, afterall, a billion dollar business and is the third largest global source of profit from organised crime. Characterised by low investments and high returns, the business of human trafficking is on a fast growth path. Given the enormity of the problem, the response of the Indian authorities in curbing trafficking has been clearly inadequate. Long, porous borders with its neighbouring countries, collusion between law enforcement agencies and traffickers, and widespread economic disparities have given India the dubious distinction of being a source, transit and destination country of trafficking of women and children from both within and outside the country. The report has also faulted India's Central Government for its inadequate and uneven efforts to prevent victims of trafficking. The Department of Women and Child Development (DWCD), the nodal office coordinating an anti-trafficking programme, is constrained by lack of resources and the fact that the State government is responsible for the implementation of the programme. In the light of UNIFEM funded report on trafficking in India, prepared by the National Human Rights Commission and the Institute of Social Sciences, has found that 40 per cent of police officials are unaware of the growing trade in women and children, and in fact, one out of two police officers does not treat this issue as a priority. (Rozario, 1988).

While the government is grappling with the problem, the

situation has worsened further. The UNIFEM funded report states categorically that India is one of the worst-affected countries as far as trafficking of women and children is concerned. Rough estimates suggests that the number of trafficked persons ranges between two to three million. Women and children are among the worst victims as they are far more vulnerable to exploitation and sexual abuse. There are only fragmented studies on the issue as most cases of trafficking go unreported. Statistics or no statistics, there is no denying the fact that the situation in Indian subcontinent is very grim. This was commented by UNDP's Meera Mishra, policy consultant on trafficking. There are several women who leave their poverty-stricken villages when promised well-paid jobs in cities, but once they reach their destination, they are promptly pushed into sex trade by ruthless traffickers. Women from India are trafficked to the Middle East, again with the promise of well-paid jobs, but invariably find themselves living like bonded labourers. Their passports are ceased, they are denied their proper amount of wages, beaten with brooms and rods and even face the sexual violence if they try to escape. The inter-State trafficking is on the rise, according to Shakti Vahini, a NGO, working in the area of trafficking, while the cross-border trafficking has contributed for the occurrences of various kinds of crisis within the country. Young girls from drought-prone areas like Andhra Pradesh are being sold to brothel owners in cities or to farm owners for use as cheap labour. The rampant practice of female foeticide in the northern States of Haryana and Punjab has fuelled internal trafficking. Since, there is a shortage of women in these States because of a low ratio of females to that of males, they have become a fertile ground for the trafficking operations. The traffickers procure girls from far away States like Assam and Orissa, conveys false hopes to their families into believing that these girls are to be married and within the garb of marital knot these girls are in no time pushed into sex trade. Trafficking has existed for ages and has increased over time, it has undergone fundamental changes in recent times. *Trafficking happens in the context of movement of people. Earlier it was associated with coercion but in the past few years, more and more women have been moving out voluntarily to look for livelihood in this process, however, they are lured, coerced, duped and pushed into sex-selling business.* This is what happens as explained by Mishra. While unequal growth and distribution of wealth remains the primary reason for this large-scale trafficking, the low-status afforded to women in patriarchal societies has also contributed to the problem. (Rozario, 1988)

The circuit of relationship between the sex workers, their clients and pimps in Kolkata zone. In the city of Kolkata, six different classes of sex workers has been identified. Those who solicit standing on the roadside or on the lanes belong to the lowest rung. Majority of the sex workers inhabits in the dark, filthy, dingy rooms in the slums catering the clients who are mostly porters and poor *chotolok* (men of lowest social and economic status). The next higher level is occupied by those who lives in two-storeyed *mathkota* or mud-build house. These sex workers can be seen in the *Malapara Lane*, *Dacca Patti* and *Jora Bagan* area. Generally, *gadiwalla* (business man), shopkeeper and lower grade staff of the rich are the frequent customers. In gradation domicile, next comes the sex workers who live in the one-storeyed brick-built or *pukka* building. They are better in appearance, behaviour and more charming than the other two groups mentioned before. The better off among them live in *Chitpur Road*, *Harkata Gali* and *Haripadmini Gali* and their clients are mostly clerks. Then there is a class of sophisticated sex workers considered as the highest of the lot and there are two types within this category. One of them is *bandha* (permanent) while the other is *chooto* (occasional). The former entertains regular visitors and the latter is more proficient in singing and dancing. The highest category of sex workers can be seen mainly in *Sonagachi* and they are also proficient in art and education. The kept-mistress and street walker forms another category of sex workers. The rich men who can afford to pay the mistress regularly keep them in homes as wives but this is temporary though cases of lifelong union are quite common. The street walkers are sex workers of the lower rung and they suffer from miserable conditions. In evening, they resort to streets dressed in garish finery with a hope to find a client. Most of them are soiled and carrier of diseases and few of them even have connection with the thieves and their clients mainly constitute the criminals of the under-world. (Joarder, 1985)

In Bio-Med Center (BMC) International Health and Human Rights Report, 2006; the demographic characteristics of Female Sex Workers (FSWs) have been summarised. The age range of FSWs was 16 to 54 years [standard deviation (SD) 6.33 years] with mean age of 27.8, 26.0, and 24.7 years for the street-home-brothel based FSWs, respectively. On comparing the age distribution between FSWs and women aged 15 to 54 years in Andhra Pradesh, the proportion of those between 20 to 34 years was significantly higher among FSWs (75.6%) than in the women population of Andhra Pradesh (45.3%). The proportion of brothel-based FSWs was highest in the 20-24 years age group (37.4%) followed by home based FSWs (31.5%) as compared with the women in Andhra Pradesh (16.1%) and the proportion of street based FSWs was highest among the 25-29 years age group (30.8%) as compared with 16.4% among the women in Andhra Pradesh. (Table 7.2)

The non-street-based FSWs, illiterate, living in small urban towns, and who started sex work at the age of 12–15 years were more likely to be in sex work for more than 5 years. The mean duration of sex work was the least for street-based FSWs. This finding reinforces the fact that the turnover of FSWs is relatively more among the street based as compared with the non-street-based FSWs. The street-based FSWs are the *informal* (unorganized) sex workers as compared with non-street-based FSWs who are more organized. In our study, the proportion of FSWs who had worked as sex workers for the

Table 7.2 : Distribution of Demographic Characteristics for the Three Types of Female Sex Workers

		Type of female sex workers				
Variable	*Variable Categories*	*Street-based (N=5010) Number (% of N)*	*Home based (N=1499) Number (% of N)*	*Brothel-based (N=139) Number (% of N)*	*Total-(N=6648) Number (% of N)*	*Chi-square test for Trend*
Age group (years)	16-19	409 (8.2)	233(15.5)	28(20.1)	673(10.1)	$p<0.0001$
	20-24	1215(24.3)	472(31.5)	52(37.4)	1739(26.2)	
	25-29	1541(30.8)	365(24.3)	27(19.4)	1933(29.1)	
	30-34	1087(21.7)	251(16.7)	18(12.9)	1356(20.4)	
	35-39	538(10.7)	124(8.3)	12(8.6)	674(10.1)	
	40-44	182(3.6)	43(2.9)	1(0.7)	226(3.4)	
	45-49	35 (0.7)	10(0.7)	1(0.7)	46(0.7)	
	50-54	3 (0.1)	1(0.1)	0	4(0.1)	
Caste*	Forward	256(5.1)	64(4.3)	13(9.4)	333(5.0)	$p<0.0001$
	Backward	1808(36.1)	910(60.7)	89(64.0)	2807(42.2)	
	Scheduled Caste	1946(38.8)	381(25.4)	23(16.5)	2350(35.3)	
	Scheduled Tribe	649(13.0)	46(3.1)	3(2.2)	698(10.5)	
	*Not Applicable	349(7.0)	98(6.5)	11(7.9)	458(6.9)	
Education Level	Illiterate	3851(76.9)	1017(67.8)	98(70.5)	4966(74.7)	$p<0.0001$
	Primary Education (I to V)	862(17.2)	318(21.2)	27(19.4)	1207(18.2)	
	More than Primary Education	297(5.9)	164(10.9)	14(10.1)	475(7.1)	
Marital Status	Currently married	2280(45.5)	394(26.3)	24(17.3)	2698(40.6)	
	Separated	1539(30.7)	347(23.1)	37(26.6)	1923(28.9)	$p<0.0001$
	Divorced	82(1.6)	35(2.3)	1(0.7)	118(1.8)	
	Widowed	642(12.8)	139(9.3)	11(7.9)	792(11.9)	
	Never Married	467(9.3)	584(39.0)	66(47.5)	1117(16.8)	
Number of living children	None	890(17.8)	585(39.0)	71(51.5)	1546(23.3)	$p<0.0001$
	1	1035(20.7)	275(18.3)	23(16.5)	1333(20.1)	
	2	1684(33.6)	349(23.3)	25(18.0)	2058(31.0)	
	>2	1401(28.0)	290(19.3)	20(14.4)	1711(25.7)	

* Not applicable for those belonging to religion other than Hindu.
Separated—Not staying with husband but not legally divorced

majority of the 12 months were higher among the non-street-based as compared with street-based FSWs. The mean age at starting sex work for FSWs from rural areas was lower to those in the large urban areas. Related to this, the gap between the first vaginal intercourse and that in exchange for money was also the least for FSWs in rural areas and the most for those in large urban areas.This finding highlights that the economic opportunities for women in rural areas are relatively less than those in the urban areas, and hence, the former get into sex work earlier than the latter.

Interestingly, the mean age at first vaginal intercourse was similar for the different types of FSWs but the gap between the first vaginal intercourse and that in exchange for money was less for non-street-based FSWs. The proportion of FSWs having a gap of more than 5 years between first vaginal intercourse and that in exchange for money was higher among the street-based FSWs as compared with the non-street based FSWs, thereby, highlighting that the former get involved with sex work later and hence are more likely to be adult women as compared with the latter. As the street-based FSWs were also more likely to be currently married/separated/divorced as compared with the non-street-based FSWs, it can be speculated that their impetus to get into sex work is to contribute to family income and they could, in some cases, be the sole supporters of their families.

In the background of increasing numbers of women infected with HIV, there is a need to address the specific factors that contribute to women's vulnerability and risk. This increased risk of HIV in women is also a reflection of gender inequalities.

The National AIDS Control Organization (NACO) is responsible for the national HIV/AIDS programme in India. NACO envisions that targeted interventions among the high-risk populations that include behaviour change,health care, treatment of sexually-transmitted diseases, provision of condoms, and creating an enabling environment for behaviour change are an effective way of reducing HIV/AIDS . On the other hand, it is now well established that HIV/AIDS is a broad development issue and not merely a disease and that it is not just a problem of individual behaviour but is influenced by social, economic, cultural marginalisation and gender inequality. Extrapolations of data from our study suggest that many women enter sex work due to economic reasons.These economic reasons, in turn, are associated with illiteracy,lower status in the society, limited economic options for women, and separation/divorce from husband or death of husband in case of married women.

Therefore, it is difficult to envisage a decrease in the numbers of women affected with HIV/AIDS unless the basic factors that contribute to women's vulnerability and risk of HIV are addressed. NACO has many partnerships and collaborations for HIV/AIDS prevention programmes, including that with the Department of Family Welfare (DoFW) that is responsible for provision of maternal and child care services and population control. However, no clear linkages are established with the Department of Women and Child Development (DoWCD), the mandate of which is to empower women both economically and socially to become equal partners in national development along with men through provision of welfare and support services, training for employment and income generation, awareness generation and gender sensitization. It would seem prudent to have effective collaboration between NACO and DoWCD for a holistic long-term approach to deal with HIV/AIDS, with special focus on women who are aged 21–34 years, illiterate,and belonging to scheduled caste and scheduled tribe.

The legal status of sex work has significant bearing on the effectiveness of HIV/AIDS programmes targeting sex workers. In India, the legal context of sex work is quite complex, and FSWs are held by police under the *ImmoralTraffic Prevention Act* that deals with human trafficking. There are indications that the present laws tend to penalize FSWs and not the exploiters or clients even though prostitution by itself is not a crime under this Act [6, 22].

More often that not, such legal structure results in making the already invisible sex worker populations more inaccessible to HIV prevention programmes, decrease the availability of health care services for them, and increase the risk of violence. Therefore, attempts have to be made to change the unfavourable legal environment for these women to increase their access to the wide range of support services, including HIV prevention. Effective collaboration between NACO, law-makers and implementers,and DoWCD are needed to achieve such a change in the environment.

Sociological Concepts Embedded Within Sexual Labour

The rise of patriarchy can be traced right from the advent of the institution of family. The word *patriarchy* literally means the rule of the father or the *patriarch* which is in common parlance is characterised as male domination. The nature of patriarchy differs from one historical epoch to the other and it is shaped by the particular culture. The broader principles of patriarchy to subordinate women remains the same but it throws up its variation in different castes and class. Patriarchy is embedded in both social structure as well as in ideology that systematically ushers in the domination of male over female. Today, media and even educational institutions spread patriarchal ideology by showing men to be stronger in decision-making positions and women as voracious consumers, dependant and jealous (Bhasin, 2003). Ideology plays an important role in giving a social shape to a particular context or a terminology. It can be identified that the following areas can be said to be under patriarchal control, *women's productive or labour power*; *women's reproduction*; *women's sexuality*; *women's mobility*; *property and other economic resources*; *social, cultural and political institutions*. (Bhasin, 2003). Considering the above aspects, it can be identified that the major social institutions such as family, religion, law, political, economic, media, and knowledge systems are all patriarchal in nature and are pillars of the patriarchal structure. The deep-rooted existence of patriarchy within these social institutions, therefore, makes patriarchy inevitable. The issue of violence can also be constructed under patriarchy. It is not the fact that women are powerless and continue in unequal participation within patriarchy but it surely does not obliterate the fact that the system itself is a male-dominated one. (Bhasin, 2003)

The Hindu scriptural texts claims that at the dawn of the creation women emerged as sinful creatures, fire, snakes and poison all rolled into one. The author of *Dharmashastra*, Manu, argues that at the moment of creation itself, women were allotted the habits of lying, sitting around, with an indiscriminate love for ornaments, and qualities such as anger, meanness, treachery and bad conduct. Manu further notes; *knowing their disposition, which the Lord of creatures laid on them at creation (i.e., their reproductive power, their sexuality, their essential nature), every man should most strenuously exert himself to guard them*. The ancient Greeks who worshipped both gods and goddesses were convinced that men were the measure of perfection, while women were fundamentally imperfect. The philosopher Aristotle holds that women are naturally lacking in intelligence and rationality. Their bodies lack the necessary warmth that make for human intelligence. It is because they are the natural fools, women do not deserve to be citizens who could participate in public affairs. They are to leave these matters to their men who could represent their interest better. Buddhist texts holds the view that woman's innate nature is somewhat calamitous. A *Jataka* tale states that women as a sex symbol are unable to differentiate truth from the falsehood and lies from truth. They are unstable as the sand, venomous like snake. Another similar text holds that women are wrathful, slanderous, integrates sewer of strife and dissension. The very nature of women demands that they be controlled and disciplined by men. Christianity maintains that God created man first, and woman next (from man's rib) and, therefore, seeks to prove man as an exemplary figure whereas women are the secondary and dependent being. Islam too believes that men were created to rule over and manage the lives and affairs of women. Islam also associates women's body with impurity. Going to the toilet on a journey, being sick and touching women are all considered equally impure acts. Those who have done any of these things are enjoined not to pray until they have washed themselves. The religious explanation of masculinity and femininity are historical in nature. They evolved over a period of time and several meanings are attached to it. Very early in the prehistoric period human beings have been awed and perplexed by the phenomenon of birth and the very birth seemed miraculous and seemed that only women knew about it. Nevertheless, once men learnt to domesticate animals, they realised that they too played a significant role in procreation. Therefore, men were eager to explain motherhood and birth in a way which did not concede too much power to women. Men came up with various explanations to subjugate women saying that women are inferior because their bodies are unclean. Ancient Hebrew texts suggested that *seed* should be compared to that of *semen* as a source of child's soul and women was merely the substrate where it was sown. This is how men denied woman's power over birth. (*Geeta*, 2002)

The religious texts are one of the very important sources for the shaping up the ideology of a civilisation. Moreover, the culture of each civilisation varies with the diverse dimensions of ideology. Therefore, the systematic subordination of women mentioned within the religious texts are the precipitating factors of present day women's subjugation within the society.

We can explain violence as a brutal force existing within the patriarchal framework which serves as a means of controlling and subjugating women located within the framework. The issue of violence attributed against women is, therefore, manifold and hence, their manifestations take place in varied ways. The terminology *violence* has been defined in many ways by the legal, professional and those defined by the concerned women. The legal definition refers to an authority which police and courts of law are able to intervene. They frequently try to obscure physical violence. The professional definition relies more on the evidences that proves the acts and also tries to impose certain meaning upon individuals. The definitions of violence by women are different from the rest. Within the feminist perspectives there are various strands. Radical feminists believe that there should not be any predetermination with the meaning of the term *violence* and see the term through feminist lens. They treat *sexual violence* as a different kind of violence because the very act is directed against women's bodies which is socially treated as sexual. The advent of the feminist theories has refuted the age-old androcentric theories or the male-stream theories which were patriarchal in nature. The belief of treating violence as a *normal* or *natural* phenomena was challenged by the views of feminist theories. The issue of *violence* can be explained within the various schools of thought located in the feminist discourse.

The traditional *marxists* theorists believe in the existence of exploitative relations of production based on extraction and appropriation of surplus labour which are the determining factors of all forms of social oppression and exploitation, including male domination over women. The domination and subjugation of women by men is located within the capitalist mode of production. Women are treated as *industrial reserve army*; a special group of labour who would provide cheap labour and perform the bulk of unpaid *reproductive* labour at home but the traditional Marxist thinkers fails to locate the domestication of female labour. The concept of *private property* was, therefore, identified by the traditional Marxists as enemy and not patriarchy; and to them, the emergence of private property has led to the constant exploitation of women.They view the patriarchal exploitation within the framework of class oppression. They argue about the domestication of labour and identify the fact that women's domestic work is not trivialised and the women's work is not considered as that of the *real work*.

The *radical feminist* viewpoint arose as a response against the Marxist-feminist approach who stressed on the fact that patriarchy is the sole enemy. The radical feminists saw the modern technology as a saviour from child bearing and consequently from exploitation. According to them, patriarchy is the systematic and institutionalised practice of violence against women, the issue of domination over women. The band of violence from that of the motherhood and control of women's bodies by male-dominated medicine, rape, sexual abuse, wife battering, incest, molestation, pornography and others should be confronted by the rejection of any life relations with men and making a community devoid of men.

The *liberal feminists* believes equality among the two gender need to be established. They firmly hold that in a male-dominated society women should work her way up to establish equality between men and women. They say that it is absolutely wrong to have an idea that women lacks rationality and, therefore, they should not be prevented from participation in public, political life. They feel that women's liberation could be brought about only through legal measures.

The occurrences of violence within brothels often go unnoticed as legal structure and the officials tend to ignore the issue of violence within the brothel itself. The first and foremost occurrences of violence takes place in the form of *rape*. The term rape can be defined as non-consensual intercourse through the use of physical force, threats or coerciveness. The phenomenon of rape can occur between two people who know each other or those who were previously in consensual sexual relationship. The very act of rape creates physical as well as mental trauma to the victim especially if it is done within the known space where the victim survives. More often, the sex workers are subjected to unwanted sexual abuses where woman is forced to have sexual intercourse with the person who abused her before or the woman is cajoled to take part in unwanted sexual acts. Besides, the psychological plight that results from constant verbal abuse, unnecessary harassment, deprivation of the required resources and destruction of personal possession, which I refer as *sexuality*.

The Sex Workers and Law: An Indian Context

The Indian Penal Code that emerged in 1860 was drafted by

Indian Law Commission with Macaulay at its helm of affairs. However, it was later revised by a Committee headed by Sir Barnes Peacock, a later Law Member of India. In his draft, Macaulay devoted clauses 254 to 362 of chapter XVIII, on offences against human body.

Here, I will closely scrutinise the concept *rape* as an offence against human body. Macaulay devoted clauses 359 and 360 to the offence of rape. From a reading of clause 359, one arrives at the following conclusions. First, there is an unmistakable preference of the rights of husband over his wife against wife's rights to herself. This is why, the wife was not entitled to accuse her husband of rape, whatever may be the real circumstances demanded. Second, a married woman could claim that she had given her consent because she was mistaken about the man's identity. If she is not married, she had no right to give her consent to any person whatsoever; the fact that she gave it was sufficient to acquit the man.

When dealing with the cases of rape the courts are likely to take into consideration facts about the victim— such as her character, age and experience— while determining the severity of punishment, and rightly so. Women of low caste in India, whose economic status was as low as their social status, did not find it easy to evade assaults on them by men of the more powerful social groups. Instead of assuring equal protection of the law for all, the Commission was only reinforcing the caste system and its rigid hierarchy.

The term *consent* is misused in many ways. If a woman's consent is proved, then there is no rape. If woman is without character, it is easier to infer that her consent was given than otherwise. But what matters more than her status is her actual conduct, and her status can only be a minor component in determining a conduct. The fact that a woman's character is relevant in determining whether or not rape was committed should not blind us to the fact that, should the offence be proved, the offence itself is against society and should be punished as such. (Dhagamwar, 1992)

Victorian morality was very much in evidence in clause 359. An unmarried or widowed woman who gave her consent was obviously without character and, therefore, could not be raped by deception. Yet matrimony was no proof that the woman was of good character and the question was open to factual proof. It is significant that although the law commissioners disagreed on the quantum of punishment for rape, they both saw the problem in terms of a high caste woman's violation by low caste men as the most heinous of rapes, requiring the strictest punishment. On the question of rape, very strong and moral judgements were brought to bear upon the victim and her character before she could obtain justice. (Dhagamwar, 1992)

The following data enumerates the various penal provisions of the *Suppression of Immoral Traffic in Women and Girls Act* and the punishment provided for each offence. Section 3(1), the offence is *keeping or managing or acting or assisting in the keeping or management of a brothel* and the punishment says that there are two convictions. The first conviction says about *imprisonment for a term of not less than one year and not more than three years and also with a fine exceeding to Rs. 2,000*. Second conviction, *imprisonment for a term of not less than two years and not more than five years and also with a fine exceeding to Rs. 2,000*. Here, the section reveals that one cannot run or administer brothels or be a part of it. Even assisting and becoming part of the brothel is punishable by law. The punishments are similar except that in the first one there is imprisonment for maximum three years while in the latter it is for the maximum period of five years.

Section 3(2), the offence is *using or allowing the use of premises as a brothel of which the accused is the tenant, lessee, occupier or person in charge, or, being the landlord, owner or lessor of any premises or being the agents of such owner, lessor or landlord and letting the premises or any part thereof with the knowledge that the same is intended to be used as brothel*. There are two punishments, the first conviction holds that, *imprisonment for a term extending to two years and fine extending to Rs. 2,000*; the second conviction says that, *imprisonment for a term extending to five years and also with a fine*. This law defines that using any house and turning it into a brothel is punishable under law. It also states the fact that the tenant, lessee, occupier or person in charge, are all liable to be punished under this law.

Section 4, the offence is *knowingly living on the earnings of prostitution*; and the punishments is *imprisonment for a term extending two years or fine extending to Rs. 1,000 or both*. Here, if one lives and draws its sustenance from the earnings of a sex trade knowingly it is punishable but the same if it is done unknowingly is not to be punished.

Section 5, the offence is *procuring, inducing or taking a woman or girl for prostitution*; and the punishment that is to be granted is *first, imprisonment for a term of not less than one year and not more than two years and also with fine extending to Rs. 2,000; second, imprisonment for a term of not less than two years and also fine extending to Rs. 2,000*. This law makes an argument for the issue of trafficking and forced sex trade. Here, if dealt carefully the pimps can be convicted along with the traffickers.

Section 6, the offence is *detaining women or girls in a brothel or premises where prostitution is carried on*. The punishment that is extended is similar to the above one. This law is like a continuation of the previous law, as this refers to more of the business of forced sex trade where women and girls are brought into and then they are unable to escape from there.

Section 7(1), the offence states that *prostitution is or in the vicinity of a public place, and the punishment is imprisonment up to three months*. This law however suggests that sex trade is punishable only when it occurs within the vicinity of the public domain. This law is indirectly suggesting that if the brothels are built in far away places then it is not a legal offence. Section 7(2) is similar to that of 3(2).

Section 8, the offence is *seducing or soliciting in a public place for the purpose of prostitution*, and the punishment is *imprisonment up to six months or fine up to Rs. 500 or both.*

Section 9, the offence noted is *seducing a woman or girl or causing or aiding or abetting her seduction when she is in the custody of the accused*, and the punishments are, *first, imprisonment for a term of not less than one year and not more than three years and also fine up to Rs. 1,000; second, imprisonment up to five years and also fine up to Rs. 1,000.*

Section 11(4), the offence is *failure to notify residence or change of or absence from such residence required under this section*, and the punishment is *fine up to Rs. 250.*

(Raghuramaiah, 1991, pp. 52-54)

In attempt to evaluate the above laws that exist for the protection against the act of trafficking, I have found that there exists flaw within the laws itself. The law stated in the article 3(1) seems to contradict the clause mentioned in the article 7(1). If the brothel management is banned or rather illegal in the eyes of law then it cannot suggest that if it is not carried out in the vicinity of a public place it is not punishable under law. So, the latter clause indirectly supports the act of brothel management in an invisible manner. The subtle language changes in the formation of legal statements denies the justice to the girl who have been kidnapped or is induced into the phenomenon of sex trade forcefully. Section 4 seems to be very vague when required to be analysed extensively. When the helpless poor mother of a sex-worker depends on her daughter for mere sustenance and is left with no other option, this law is quite crucial in this case. In the same case, the dependant can be suffered from acute diseases like cancer, HIV positive syndrome, or other venereal diseases; especially, when the law does not mention a ban on sex trade rather it only specifies that it should be away from the public places. In this regard, I shall also like to bring about the reference of Part V (Articles 17-22) of Committee on the Elimination of Discrimination Against Women (CEDAW). The UN General Assembly adopted CEDAW on December 18, 1979. President Jimmy Carter signed it in 1980. The Senate Foreign Relations Committee passed it on September 29, 1994, but the full Senate has not ratified it. So far, 165 countries have signed the treaty, legally binding them to implement its provisions. After signing, each country must submit an initial report with a detailed and comprehensive description of the state of its women. This initial report is said to include legislative, judicial, administrative and other measures the signatory nation has adopted to comply with CEDAW. Treaty provisions also includes Legalised Prostitution. Article 11, Section 1(c) of the treaty upholds, *the right to free choice of profession and employment*. The Committee has included voluntary prostitution in that free choice.

The Prevention of Immoral Trafficking in Person was passed by the Indian Parliament in 1986 which was an amendment to the suppression of the Immoral Traffick in Women and Girls Act. The change in the word from *suppression* to *prevention* widened the scope of the Act. Then, the words such as *women* and *girls* were also replaced by the term *persons* and this indicated inclusion of not only females but also men and eunuchs who were also trafficked for sex trade. At a definitional level, the act brought about a number of changes from a female offering her body for promiscuous sexual intercourse for hire whether in money or kind to the sexual exploitation or abuse of persons for commercial purposes. The widened meaning allowed any form of sexual exploitation or abuse. This broader definition of a brothel made it easier to persecute those keepers of brothels for all kinds of sexual abuse and exploitation which may not amount to sexual intercourse alone. (Chatterjee, 2,000)

Section 375 of the Indian Penal Code explains rape in the following way : *penetration is sufficient to constitute the sexual intercourse necessary to the offence of rape.* A man is said to have committed rape according to this section, if he has sexual intercourse with a woman in circumstances falling under any of the six following descriptions; *against her will; without her consent; with her consent when the consent has been obtained by putting her or any person in whom she is interested, in fear of death or hurt; with her consent if it is given because she believes the man to be her lawfully married husband, when the man knows he is not; with her consent if she is unable to recognise the nature and consequences of that to which she gives consent because of intoxication or unsoundness of mind; with or without her consent if she is under sixteen years of age.*

(Menon, 2000)

The language of the laws are binded within the patriarchal framework and if we compare the language of the present day laws to those which existed during the colonial rule, we will find that there have been several amendments. Despite the amendments, the structure remains embedded within the patriarchy. In the pre-British era, sex workers enjoyed the property rights. There were *baijis* (who were the singers and used to entertain rich zamindars) and they received huge amount of money from the landlords and also property. The colonial era declared the sex trade as illegal and, therefore, confiscated the property of the sex workers. As a result, the profession continued somehow but legally their right of possession of property has been curbed down dragging them into more and more suppression. The Indian Penal Code has been structured over the years but the granting of economic rights and possession of property to the sex workers have never been allowed.

Inferences

My first observation is that there are flaws within the legal statements itself which fails to locate the severity of the problem. Lawyers and judges are reluctant to the issues of violence and other exploitation carried out in the brothels. The law does not clearly mentions the role of pimps and brothel owners, so the exploitation within it continues.

Since, the institution of sex trade exists from the time immemorial people believe that it is a natural part of our society. There are various debates concerning its abolition. The exploitation happening within the institution itself is changing day by day, it has worsened further, and violence has increased if we trace the trajectory of the growth of the institution of the sex trade itself. If we see Indian literature, we will find that mention was made about the profession where the sex trade continued within the means of entertainment in the king's courts. But the present day act differs a great deal from that of the ancient era. The patriarchal nature of ruling however ignores the fact of violence within the sex trade itself. It is here, that the legal structure creates the problem with the word *consent* for it seeks to maintain the patriarchal stature.

The violence that is associated with this profession if often obscured by the officials such as law makers, judges, lawyers and keepers of the law such as the police. The laws that I have scrutinised so far do not take into account the violence involved within the brothels. It is as if something is quite evident that perpetrators of violence do and, therefore, the mention might be necessarily ignored.

The power of sexual politics that exists within the brothel itself also needs a mention. For, the sexual labour is over exploited and their status is reduced to mere slaves because the conditions that exists within the sex trade demean the status of those who are serving as sexual labour and the *sex* as a commodity in the sex market is constantly devalued along with the human person.

The aspect of conjugality is quite common in the brothels, therefore, the traumatic experience of the sex workers within the brothels remain absolutely unquestioned under law. The law can take care of the physical abuse or violence but there should be separate laws for the occurrences of violence particularly within the brothel itself.

To sum the whole issue, therefore, I would like to devote my conclusion here. International studies have clearly indicated that sex trade is a universal phenomenon. It has not received priority consideration in many developing countries due to a variety of factors, e.g., in patriarchal set-up of a country where the rulers and law makers are males, problems of utmost urgency, crucial to women are bypassed as secondary. The problem of sex trade is often viewed superficially, not in its reality and pushed aside as trivial. Besides, due to the general acceptance of sex trade by society this problem is considered common. Sex trade can be identified as a problem because the value any society places on women, the roles attributed to them, their position and status in society are undoubtedly crucial factors in this matter. International Abolitionist Federation's Sex Trade: Survival of Slavery states that to accept sex working as a profession (willingly or under stress) is a totally retrograde step depriving women of their independence, privacy and above all, human dignity, and reducing them to the level of servitude. Sex trade and the accompanying evil of the traffic in persons for the purpose of sex trade are incompatible with the dignity and worth of the human person and endanger the welfare of the individual, the family and the community. Untruthful love and pseudo-relationships, egoism and selfishness, degradation and contempt for women are distortions of reality. In any society, the image of women is consistent with the way men wants to see and use them. The sexual act, an expression of mutual love between marital partners tends to be reduced to an animal operation devoid of tenderness, affection and truthful love. The most alarming fact, however, in the contemporary world, is that in complete disregard for all human and international laws, the flesh-traders indulge in trafficking children. The problem that I wish to establish here is that the phenomena of sex trade both in India as well as in Global perspective is a vicious web which remain congruent to that of a cage which provides an easy entry but a perilous exit.

Notes

- In my analysis, I have used the term *sex worker* instead of *prostitute*; but, the term prostitute has been used in places where reference has been made with the specific text and author. I prefer to use the term sex worker as they are a part of the unorganised labour sector.
- I wanted to establish the fact with regard to the nature of this profession, i.e., it corresponds to that of a cage where a prey is given a very warm welcome and is captured forever.
- I also questioned that how far the sex workers enjoys their freedom of work, with periodic sexual assaults and tyranny of owners, customers and to some extent their peers.

References

Abbott, Pamela, *et al.*, 1997, *An Introduction to Sociology: Feminist Perspectives*, Routledge.

Allsebrook, A. and Swift, A., 1989, *Broken Promise*, London: Hodder and Stoughton.

Altman, Dennis, 2001, *Global Sex*, University of Chicago Press.

Balen, B., Kevin, 2005, *Understanding Global Slavery: A Reader*, Routledge Publisher.

Barry, L, Kathleen, 1995, *The Prostitution of Sexuality*, New York University Press.

Bernstein, Elizabeth, *et al.*, 2004, *Regulating Sex: The Politics of Intimacy and Identity*, Routledge.

Bishop, Ryan, *et al.*, 1998, *Night Market: Sexual Cultures and Thai Economic Miracle*, Routledge.

Burgess, Wolbert, Ann, *et al.*, 1996, *Understanding Violence against Women*, National Academic Press.

Chatterjee, Ratnabali, 2000, *Marching by Candle Light*,University of Calcutta:Women's Studies Research Centre.

Chattopadhyay, Aparna, 2003, *The Institution of Devadasis*, Baroda Oriental Institute.

Dank, Michael, Barry, 1999, *Sex Work and Sex Workers*, Transaction Publisher.

Dworkin, Andrea, 1987, *Intercourse*, Arrow Book.

Ehrenreich, Barbara, *et al*, 2003, *Global Women: Nannies, Maids and Sex Workers in the New Economy*, New York: Metropolitan Books.

Fausboll, 1981, *Indian Mythology*, New Delhi: Cosmo Publication.

Hoigard, Cecilie, *et al.*, 1992, *Backstreets: Prostitution, Money and Love*, Polity Press.

Joarder, B, 1985, *Prostitution in 19th and early 20th century*, Inter-India Publications.

John, Mary, 1998, *Globalisation, Sexuality and the Visual Field: Issues and Non-issues for Cultural Critique in Mary John*, et al., (ed.), A *Question of Silence: The Sexual Economies of Modern India*, New Delhi:Kali for Women.

Jordan, K. Kay, 2003, *From Sacred Servant to Profane Prostitute*, Manohar Publishers, New Delhi.

Kempadoo, Kamala, *et al.*, 1998, *Global Sex Workers: Rights and Resistance*, Routledge.

Lim, Lean Lin, 1998, *The Sex Sector: The Economic and Social bases of Prostitution in South-East Asia*, International Labour Organisation.

Mackenzie, A. Donald, 2004, *Indian Myth and Legend*, Gresham Publishing Company, London.

Manderson, Lenore, 2003, *Violence Against Women in Asian Societies*, Routledge.

Menon, Nivedita, 2000, Embodying the Self: Feminism, Sexual Violence and the Law in Partha Chatterjee, *et al*, (ed.), *Subaltern Studies XI: Community, Gender and Violence*, Permanent Black and Ravi Dayal.

Posner, A. Richard, 1992, *Sex and Reason*, Harvard University Press, USA.

Raghuramaiah, Lakshmi, K. 1991, "Night Birds, Indian Prostitutes", *From Devadasis to Call Girls*, Chanakya Publications.

Ringdal, Johan Nils, 2004, *Love for Sale: A World History of Prostitution*, Grove Press, New York..

Rozario, Sr. R.M., 1988, *Trafficking in Women and Children in India*, Uppal Publishing House, New Delhi.

Reports

Coomaraswamy, Radhika, 1995, *Violence Against Women*, Indian Association of Women's Studies.

Dondona, Rakhi, *et al.*, 2006, Demography and Sex Work Characteristics of Female Sex Workers in India, BMC International Health and Human Rights, *http://creativecommons.org/licenses/by/2.0* accessed on 12/07/2009.

8
Women behind Bars

R. G. Dastidar

The present article is based on the study done on women prisoners of Bhopal Central Jail. The study focused on various issues of sociological relevance and an attempt is made to read the situation in gender theories. Some of the data have been presented here by case study method. Abstracts of the field notes have been left in the racy style they were first written in especially, so that the actual import of life in jails is not lost to the reader. It attempts to document the lives of women inmates in the jail and in doing so it also reflects on the jail system, its administration, our legal system and societal conception of justice at large and women's position thereof. The study is situated in the feminist dialogue inadvertently because, ultimately jails tend to function as "a society" and the tools of feminist perspective find effective use there. Although jails tend to be isolationist and removed from the society, they continue to be reflections of free society in a more brutally honest fashion. This study found a pattern to women criminality, which ultimately reflects patriarchal values, which, it is hoped subsequent studies will explore further and only then perhaps some kind of theory may be evolved.

Why do women commit crime or break the law? Traditionally this was viewed under one of the non-gendered theories on sociological, psychological or genetic/biological fixation of crime. Recent works have however have shown that these theories do not wholly bring out the various compulsions, constraints and limitations of women's lives. As some recent theories would suggest some women criminals is the result of the indoctrination of gendered social structure and may be, even victims thereof, considering the final outcomes of their act and how it changes their lives. Forsaken, ignored and forgotten by friends and family women inmates live years of a meaningless existence in jails. Knowing fully well that whatever their crime they have no one to go back to. Everything in their past is lost to them and they dare not dream of any future burdened with stigma of jail, and are ultimately left without friends and family. How do they see that one defining moment which changed their lives?

Introduction

Sociology has a long history of studies on crime and justice. Sociologists have been concerned with the study of crime, criminality, societal corrective mechanisms, their efficacy and social alternatives, justice and so on. Although, to start with these were mostly concerns of administrators, but recent years have seen many different agencies taking up this concern from various viewpoints. Therefore, today jails are seen as being on crossroads. The last few years has seen a shift in the perception in the causes of criminality, dispensation of correctional institutions and also justice. Today the intervention of different social organization in jails is more obvious than it was a few years ago. A look at the changing interface between the jail and society is important from both utilitarian and academic point of view.

Jail is perceived as the last solution of all modern day society to formally control crime and deviance. It stands as our unquestionable guardian, and the justified protector of our legal system and also by its deterrent value, it seemingly upholds the moral fabric of our society. Historically it has developed from being confirmatory to reformatory. It is expected to perform as a deterrent institution, regulatory as well as reformatory. Hedonic in ancient times often the bête noire of the media and activist, romanticized in literature, glorified by the freedom fighters and the heroic sacrifices of nationalist leaders, and today also very much a part of international politics, social perceptions of jails have varied down the ages and across sections of society. Yet how effective is it as an instrument of social control? Dose it actually function as a reformatory and reorients the public opinion and the world view of its inmates in favour of justice and the social system? What is the social reality of jails?

Jail is a culture specific phenomenon. According to Emile Durkheim the nature of law has been essentially repressive and jails are responsible to actualize the negative sanctions imposed by law. Thus these sanctions are restitutional and refer to total negation of one's social being. Confinement is the negation of self to restore the faith and commitment of the criminal in favour of collective society. Grass root experiences, however, do not always subscribe to this thesis. Simple criminals are sometimes likely to become hardcore because of jail experiences. Also as has been the recent news various anti-social elements and crooks actually operate from within the jails for all kinds of nefarious activities. Thus raising serious doubts about jails as an institution. Undoubtedly the very need of jails cannot be questioned as yet, but they definitely need to be more effective in terms of maintaining human dignity and upholding societal goals. A lot of in-house commissions have gone into the problem, there is heat born down by various national and international agencies. How have the jails responded to these? In part this is answered by the way the inmates experience the jails. At the other end this has to do with societal conception of human needs and its structuring itself. Also increasingly it is about corruption and apathy on the part of functioning personnel and system limitations. Studies have shown the subculture of jails and its nexus with the outside world as a comment on the social processes.

Theories on Crime and Women

India has been home to various heterogeneous ethnic groups. This has had repercussions for the society as a whole as also for various groups within it. Various social scientists have tried to explain crime in this situation from various perspectives mostly developed in the west. Broadly there are three types of theoretical explanations of criminal behaviour according to Reid (1976) that of : (1) classical and positive theories, (2) physiological, psychiatric and psychological theories and (3) sociological theories. These theories, however, do not relate to women as a different category. Women criminality has been explained by the same theories until recently, when some changes have been made by the feminist dialogue. Some of the sociological theories are as follows :

It has been traditional with social scientists to relate criminality to poor economic conditions. "Social arrangements generally are profoundly affected by the existing system of economics, and the problems of social adjustments of society, such as crime are likewise the product of and affected by the existing economic arrangement" Vold (1958). Mannheim in a study of delinquent women demonstrated the effect of the type of housing and living conditions on delinquency rates of women. On the other hand for sociologists it is no surprise that not only individuals, but also groups should turn to crime. Government of India under the British rule passed an enactment in 1871 under which various tribes committing criminal activities were categorized as criminal tribes and organized tribal criminality was recognized as a fact. Although this enactment was repelled in 1952, this however has no continuities with any direct changes in the social system. That ever since India gained independence there have been tremendous changes in our social and economic patterns are merely coincidental. Thus no great validation of the theory has come from the Indian scene. Also looking from the western point of view, most of India is very poor, but we do not see proportional representation of the populace in crime figures. The reasons for which are many and varied. But taken together they definitely decry the economic theory of crime.

Merton propounded another theory in his reference group behaviour. "There is more frequent disjunction between goals and opportunity among the lower class strata than among the upper class strata" Merton (1967). Cohen too has shown that there is frustration among the lower classes because of their inability to achieve middle class goals that they react to middle class values by forming a culture of their own (1955). Many sociologists have used this formulation in their work in India. Freud suggested biological and psychosomatic conditioning of criminality in his theory of "penis envy", a theory not very explored today. According to some other theories, crime can be best understood in its cultural context. Engaging in certain cultural practices, which comprise essentially elements of the total life pattern of lower class culture that automatically violates certain legal norms Miller (1958). Sykes and Dmatza (1957) have shown that delinquent comes to conceive of his delinquency as being right and, therefore, has no feelings of guilt.

Studies have shown that crime does not require the reconciliation of the criminal in the criminal culture, but to some it may well be a way of life. "The fact that there were tribal panchayats who facilitated and assisted members in committing crime by maintaining a scheme of social security talks of the system of crime" Kapadia (1952). Another attempt states that, "in India the difference between the army of a prince and a gang of robbers was in the general estimation of the people, only in degree, both were driving an imperial trade Bruce (1968). Whatever be the reasons of origin of criminal tribes in other respects than crime, they remain as normal and organized as any other group. Thus to Merton, deviance is the result of the blocking of the structural means to achieve the cultural goals, for Haikerwal the criminal behaviour is the result of cultural socialization in the family and tribe. Bruce has shown how *thugs* assume "*thuggee*" culture in the garb of religion. Considering the theory that violence being unwomanly, therefore, there is fewer women criminals too does not bear out. Women dacoits of Chambal bear witiness to that. But what of the gender equation? Does crime free women from social limitations prescribed by morality, status-role, etc. and, therefore empower her? Also if crime and violence are male sources of power-status then criminal women should enjoy better status.

For example violence is seen as being a non-feminine, masculine trait, and crime and violence are more often than not intermeshed. Then does the involvement of women as perpetuators of violence change their gender position? Experience world over has been that, even where women have been partners to often violent revolutions and movements but it does not in any way enhance their position as women or resolve gender issues because the basic ideology of these movements or revolutions remain extremely masculine. For example violence has been seen in the naxal or communist regimes all of which has a lot of women in their folds. But here too they are seen to be inferior to men and not as independent commanders while the revolution takes strength from fighting inequality in society and questions its hierarchy. Then can criminality as a way of life empower women or enhance her status in any way? Phoolan Devi seems to be the only visible justifcation of this thesis. Further if the ideas of virtue and morality are seen to be exploitative, women prostitutes should be free of these and, therefore, emancipated being outside it. This thesis is not born out by facts and has been well refuted by various studies. For example Devdasi cults exist all over India. They are called *maharis* in Kerala, *natis* in Assam, *muralis* in Maharashtra, *bogans* in Andhra Pradesh, and so on. The practice of dedicating young girls to the temples may hold a pseudo religious garb but research has shown that there were other more practical considerations in the prevalence of the practice. "....thus the very women whom religion had once considered as outcastes were also the most faithful custodians of its spirit and traditions", Altekar (1956).

Brief Overview

Recent years have seen a growing body of literature on women criminals. Starting from mere mention, which women criminals found in earlier studies to statistical data it is realized that some of these studies may be theoretically interrelated.

P.K.Tarapore's Prison Reform in India (1936) and F.A. Barker's, '"The Modern Prison System in India", focused on the prison system as a system and were oblivious to gender issues. Even until Vidya Bhushan's "Prison Administration" (1970) some issues relating to women start finding passing mention. Bhanot and Mishra (1978) may be considered to be the first systematic study of female offenders in India. This was, however, preceded by many papers presented in conferences and various journals. Tyler's, 'My experiences in Indian Prison" can be seen as a unique addition to the subject.

There is scarcity of data on sex-wise composition of crime committed by women. Female participation in crime and its trends and consequences are difficult to gauge. There is, however, sex-wise data on arrests which show women prisoners to be approximately 2-3 per cent of the total prisoners population in India. Types of crime committed by women are: (1) against property (pick pocketing, shoplifting, theft, etc.), (2) against person (illegal abortion, infanticide, murder, etc.), (3) against public order (like those of rioting,) and (4) miscellaneous (like those of smuggling, gambling, drug addiction, prostitution, etc.). Data does indicate more involvement of women in crime along the second and fourth category, which has on further analysis shown her involvement in women related crimes. For example like those of dowry, girl child infanticide, murder of husband, in-law, co-wife, etc. This as feminist point out is not a mere coincident, but has to be understood along the theory of gender and patriarchy. Also there is change in the role expectation of women and opportunity structure. This has created strain and anomalies both. Recent developments have seen women increasingly involved in financial and white collared crimes.

On the other hand feminist claim that women are over represented in petty crimes, which again is due to patriarchal bias. Another reason for increased representation of women in crime statistics is due to better statistical methods.

Study Area

Bhopal central jail is situated in Karond, which is almost on the outskirts of the city. Some public transport is available for the area; there are little facilities in terms of market. The jail campus is surrounded by staff quarters of the jail personnel and the near about area has some educational and other institutions coming up. The women's wing is situated on the one side of the jail, it is flanged by the male barracks on the one side and the administrative block on the other. Enclosed by high walls on all sides it is separated from the rest of the jail as also from the world outside. It houses three barracks, with a capacity of 18 per barrack. On the day of our first visit there were 109 inmates housed in the barracks. One visitor's-cum- T.V. hall. Toilets and bath enclosures are made at a little distance from the main block, they are constructed to allow surveillance from outside and have small doors, which do not allow privacy due to security reasons. Besides, there is an attached toilet with each barrack for night use when the barracks are locked and the inmates cannot go out to the main toilet. Like the others this toilet too is open to view from one side and has no windows. The stink due to inevitable use just has to be borne. There is a small work shed, kitchen (used only for food distribution and to make chappaties, cooked food is supplied from the male barrack) and some space for school and a crèches. Each barrack is a long hall with cement platforms 2/2.5ft wide for beds. The belongings of each inmate are kept on her allotted bed space, and consist of a few clothes, blanket, bucket, mug, plate and glass and also some toiletries. Some do have a few more things, but they are inevitably issues to fight over and are often robbed or just taken over by others, (inmates and as some alleged by the staff). Since the jails were over stuffed some of the inmates were allotted the space in-between the beds. If the inmate has a small child with her, she makes do in the same space. Lot of inmates had pasted pictures of gods on the wall space near their bed. Some family photographs may also rarely be found there. There is a closed (grilled) verandah along the barrack to which the only grilled ventilators/windows open. The cell and the campus around were painted and clean unlike the barracks, which seemed congested and shabby. A couple of dwarfed trees grow in the campus, along with some shrubs. Taken together it dose not give the impression of a friendly place, in fact its barren look demonstrates its almost antagonism to life. This is despite a small very brightly painted Kids park. The sight of some shabby women leaning against iron rod grill, staring vacantly is haunting and cannot be forgotten. Only the barracks looked like lived in, while the rest of the space had a very impersonal look. During our very many visits we got used to the usual atmosphere of bickering and shouting. It must be mentioned, we were warned that we would experience desperation and a sense of gloom on our visit to the barracks but this did not prepare us for the depression, which we actually experienced. The environment was exceedingly negative and gloomy and our feelings of the presence at that place were almost physical.

Life in Jail

The day starts early in jails, and is filled with some routine activities and mostly vacant time slots.

The strength in the jail changes on daily basis. It depends on the release of inmates on parole/ bail/release / arrest, etc. At the time of the study there were 108 inmates and 23 children in the women's wing. The children were below five years of age, and generally had no one in the outside world to take care of them. Those respondents, whose children were over six, and who did not have anyone to take care of them, are sent to institutions meant for this purpose, where they are brought up and also taught some skills and education. Policy decision exists in this area. In Bhopal SOS village for children, a NGO, does this work. Children in conflict with the law are sent to other institutions called *balniketans*, which are separate from those attended by the children of the inmates.

Day starts at 6 a.m. with a roll call. Breakfast of porridge/ roti and tea. Children and nursing mothers are given milk and bread. 7 a.m. to 8.30 a.m. is personal time. 9 a.m. onwards is devoted to cleaning. Work is allocated by the warden and includes cleaning of barracks, premises, toilets, painting, making chapattis, etc. Work is allocated by the warden and is used as another means of controlling the inmates by carrot and stick approach treatment some of the work like cleaning toilets etc is actually humiliating. 11 a.m. food is distributed. From 12.30 to 4p.m. is given to work/ skill learning (doll/ purse making, zardosi, beautician, etc., not compulsory) 4 p.m. to 4.30 p.m. free time. 5 p.m. dinner, at 7 p.m. roll call and barracks are locked.

Prisoners who have almost completed their term help the staff in running the jail. As happens in all other social systems some get it easy while others feel the pinch depending on their proximity to the staff, outside support, individual skills and also money. Rewards are few and far removed, competition is tough, and environment is depressive and harsh. Most of the inmates constantly bicker and rough up each other.

Respondent Profile

80 respondents were interviewed, (as the other 28 inmates were under trials), of whom 20 were in the 20-30 age group, 48 were 30-40 years old and 8 were 40-50 years old and 4 were above 51 years old. 58 belonged to joint families and 14 had lived in nuclear family 4 respondents had no family.44 were Hindus, 23 Muslims and 13 belonged to other categories like Christian, Sikh, and tribal. 24 were never married, 56

were married, and 14 were widowed. 20 were illiterate, 57 had some schooling, and 3 were graduates. 44 were from rural areas while 38 came from urban areas. The government policy to keep women in nearest jail has led to the inmates being mostly from in and around Bhopal (within 200 k.m.), however, there were three inmates from Betul district and one from Indore.68 had income of below Rs. 5,000 per month while 12 had above Rs. 5,000-10,000. The nature of offence is almost the first element to be studied in a prisoner's profile and is given in the Table. 8.1.

Table 8.1 : Reasons for Crime and the Number of Respondents

Sl. No.	*Offence committed/charged*	*Number of respondents*
1.	Attempt to murder	2
2.	Murder	38
3.	Prostitution	5
4.	Dowry Act	14
5.	Kidnapping	1
6.	Narcotics	12
7.	Others (theft, pick pocketing, case of conflict, etc.)	8
Total		80

A cursory glance on Table 8.1 showing reason for crime that a sizeable number of the women were charged for crimes committed within the family setting. This is not only unfortunate but also paradoxical that an institution meant for providing support, care and shelter should be the seat of crime. Why women in such a situation are compelled to or by design take extreme measures? What is it within the family that makes women commit crime? Families are the first and primary institution for women's social security and social role, then what kind of conflict or redefinitions are we moving towards.

As is obvious majority of women were in for murder ! The

victims were either family members (husband, mother-in-law, brother-in-law,co-wife,daughter-in-law, known person). Common theme was that of the other woman, or a drunken wife beater who in a drunken state is stabbed or burnt while sleeping. This shows the unreconciled tensions that have been suppressed and frustrations within families. What is it in our family system that will allow a pure-vegetarian to torch her daughter-in-law? Or allow a wife who has patiently borne the beatings and abuse of a husband for years suddenly axe him to death? It is the family male member who draws children and women as carriers into the drug trade, or into prostitution. Theory does not appropriately bring out this vulnerability of women to crime. The woman's dilemma is that she cannot defy her family and refuse its security while her actions often forced by her family circumstances may ultimately result in exactly that.

CASE-I

Seema was desperate as her husband had taken in another woman and literally threw her out of the house one night. None of her husband's family intervened though they lived next door, as they were already fighting over ownership of their ancestral land. On the spur of the moment she jumped into the well along with her three children. The hue and cry brought the villagers to their rescue, but she was the lone survivor. She is serving on the charge of killing her children. Her husband has a settled life and family with the other women. Reflecting back she mourns her children but knows that she could not have left them to anyone else's care.

CASE-II

Tabasum had a drunkard gambler for a husband. With two dependent children she started working for her so-called uncle who had been very generous in the past and lived in the same locality and ran a small pan shop. Slowly she learnt about his real trade, but there was no going back. Sometimes she travelled with him to Calcutta along with her children for delivering goods. The money was good and she needed it. She was arrested in Itarsi with two-kilogram hashish. The local cooperator bailed out her uncle. Nothing is known of her husband who seemingly left with a lot of money.

Case III

Asha is in the same jail as her mother-in-law, husband and brother-in-law. (Five family members in all). They are under trials allegedly for killing seven members of their father's brother's (*chacha's*) family over a land dispute. Her seven-month old son shares her destiny. The child looks under nourished and Asha laments not having enough to feed the baby. She defends her family very aggressively and vocally unlike her mother-in-law. They have hired a lawyer and her own paternal family too is in active support of her and her family of marriage. She hopes to get out within a year.

(Names of persons and places have been changed to maintain the confidentiality of the respondent's identity.)

Table 8.2 : Length of Sentence/Stay in Jail

Sl. No.	*Length of sentence*	*No. of respondents*
1.	Up to one year	4
2.	Over 1 year to 5 years	15
3.	Over 5 years to 10 years	28
4.	Over 10 years	33

Case IV

Sita has been in jail close to 10 years and is due to be released. The administration has written to her family about the date of her release but has received no response. She has only heard of her family's well-being from indirect sources. She will of course go to see them on release but she knows that there is no place for her in her husband's family. Her brother-in-law, sister-in-law, etc., are not about to share their ancestral house and few acres of agricultural land with her. Her own brothers and sisters are busy with their own family life and are anyway ashamed to have her; their argument is that they have marriageable daughters. She will probably be taken in by a N.G.O. and try to start life afresh. Most women do not have any thing or anywhere to go to once released are very uncertain about their future. Of the three tribal inmates one is due to be released shortly and seemed the most confident of acceptance by society after certain rituals. Tribal do not attach stigma to jails as such. She, however, never received any visitors from her family in jail due to poverty but hears from them through others. Another case, which seemed contrary to the norm, was of a women widow "anayasin", approaching her 60's, imprisoned for drug peddling who lived in a temple in a village. She was very confident of going back to her temple and old life for she refuses all charges though she has served her sentence.

Table 8.3 : Table Showing the status of visitors

Sl. No.	*Total no. of visitations from family/relative*	*No. of respondents*
1.	0-2	47
2.	3	19
3.	4	11
4.	5 or more	3

Problems of Women Prisoners

Prisons impact women more adversely than men. The reasons for this are varied and deeply embedded in our social processes and institutions. Home has greater relevance for women than men and this can be better appreciated only in the context of how women's lives are lived and their dependence on the family institution for it. Jails destroy women. The convicted women are considered defiled and the stigma is too burdensome to allow daughters and daughters-in-law to be accepted back into its folds. There are other economic and social considerations too.

The common problems faced by women inmates were same as those in most jails of India, irrespective of gender, namely those of overcrowding, poor infrastructure, corruption, poor health and nutrition, poor sanitation, poor medical and legal redressal. Like expected the situation is worse for women than men. A report of the workshop on prison reforms organized by Commonwealth Human Rights Initiative 2002 stated that the health problems faced in Madhya Pradesh prisons are far in excess of anything the outside population has to face. It goes on to state that against sanctioned capacity of prisons of 17,047 the State is holding up to 29,189 prisoners. Further many under trial prisoner's cases have not progressed beyond the different stages of trial for the past 3-6 years. (*ibid*). Lack of transparency in jail administration, moribund prison visiting system clearly exists as a contributory factor. Added to this is the new expectation due to human rights, and personnel are ill equipped without dated skills.

Problems of women inmates are further compounded, women in jail face social boycott and find themselves disserted by their families. Husbands often and sooner than later marry and move on. Children find themselves with some grand-parent or relative or step-parent all of whom are either incapable of looking after them and meeting their needs or are simply do not want to. This separation from small and dependent children and their children's homelessness is a great cause of worries, frustration and stress to women inmates. Small children sometimes find themselves living with their mother in the prison. In any case in the world outside jails without their mothers care and protection their future is jeopardized. C.H.R.I.(2002) report on prison reform states that there is constant delay in cases of women prisoners, women are lodged in jails distant from their native place making it very difficult for their family to keep in touch or visit them. All these issues were found to be true of Bhopal jail as well. Often the only family members who try to help women inmates are their parents, (which actually is very little help if parents are old and resource less), as sooner or later all others move on with their lives. Parole is not easy to arrange for them and records show few women go out on parole. It has also been reported often that no one comes to receive released women prisoners. Rehabilitation of released women prisoners socially as well as economically has proven to be a challenge. In this context it will be apt to quote Surekha Talari (2003),............ "it is the larger truth that most of the people who land up in jail are marginalized in the context of caste, economic status and sex. Further lacking legal literacy women find their rights violated at every stage. Some were even unaware of the sections under which they were imprisoned and understood about their case only when told by the warden about the same.

Certain vocational training programs are run under which women are taught embroidery work (*zardoise*), doll making, and are trained as beauticians or dais (para-medics) or are taught to make '*pappar*' or '*achar*'. It is hoped that these skills will help them in their rehabilitation. However, experience does not support this thesis. Most of the time spent in jails is vacant, inmates are not motivated enough to learn new skills, the work allocated by the warden is sometimes humiliating, and the overall environment depressive and inhuman. Also the skills promoted often require marketing facilities not available to inmates besides being low income generating. In their frustration the inmates often end up fighting and abusing one another. Discipline is an issue and can invoke harsh physical abuse. Much of this has been well documented and various committees like the Mullah Committee or Justice Krishna Iyer Committee or organizations like the Commonwealth Human Rights Initiative have gone into this however the very structure and functioning of jails has not seen any change. Reforms are much awaited. There is also the larger issue of identity. The present situation in the jail does not allow identification, the label of criminal often make women go on to dissociate with their present also sometimes with themselves. Mental disorders are a common problem.

Other health issues include poor nourishment. Bhopal jail authorities have hired the services of a dietician to work out the jail inmate menu, but it not much has been translated into practice. Women's special needs tend to be neglected and body aches are a common complaint. 63 per cent complained of such chronic aches, 52 per cent had sometime received treatment for depression.71 per cent had been treated for fever in the past three months in jail. All visitors are advised to give gifts of foods like lime during summer months.

Conclusion

Clearly the study showed that a majority of the women inmates were in jail because of some family situation, i.e., they were charged for having committed a crime against some family member or were accomplice in the crime committed by some family member or close associate; five cases were under "*Sita* Act" and 12 under narcotics. In none of the cases were women seen to be in control of their life or circumstances. Being in jail in most cases has led to the permanent loss of family and the associated stigma is something that will mark all their future identity. The problems faced by women in jail are greater than those faced by men due to gender patterning patriarchy, social stigma, poverty, lack of awareness and assertion and also lack of family support and the very way women identities are formed in society. For the same reasons along with others their rehabilitation is also more problematic *vis-à-vis* men. Ironically while a violent male may actually enhance his status and access to social goodies, a violent women ends up becoming all the more vulnerable unless her position is secured by alternate system of male support. Thus even in the sub-system her position remains dependent and inferior to that of males.

References

Ahuja, Ram. *Sociological Criminology*, New Age International Publishers, New Delhi, 1996.

Altekar, A.S. : *The Position of Women in Hindu Civilization*, Motilal Banarsi Das, Benaras. 1956.

Bhushan, Vidya. *Prison Administration in India, with Special Reference* to Uttar Pradesh. S. Chand , New Delhi, 1970.

Bruce, George. *The Stranglers, the Cult of Thuggee and its Overthrow in British India*. Harcourt Brace and World Inc., New York,1968.

Chaudhuri, A.B. *Witch Killings Amongst Santhals*, Ashish Pub. House, New Delhi,1984.

Cohen, Albert K. *Delinquent Boys : A Culture of The Gang*. Free Press, NewYork. 1955.

Diwan, Paras. Dowry and Protection to Married Women. Deep & Deep Pub., New Delhi,1987.

Haikerwal, B.S. Economic and Social Aspects of Crime in India.George Allen and Unwin Ltd., London,1934.

Kapadia, K .M., *The Criminal Tribes of India in Sociological Bulletin* l,11, March,1952.

Merton, R.K.: *Social Theory and Social Structure*, Free Press, New York, 1967.

Miller, W.B. Lower Class Culture as a Generating Milieu of Gang Delinquency in *Journal of Social issues*, Vol. 14, No. 3.

Nayar, Baldev Raj. *Violence and Crime in India: A Quantitative Study*. Macmillan India Ltd., Delhi, 1975.

Reid, Sue Titus. *Crime and Criminology*, The Drydon Press, Illinois,1976.

Vold, George B. *Theoretical Criminology*. Oxford Univ. Press, New York.1958.

9
The Efficacy of Laws in preventing Domestic Violence

Harneet Chima

Domestic Violence against wo.nan affects the lives of millions of women worldwide and cuts across cultural / religious barriers. It is prevalent in all socio-economic and educational classes. Violence against women is a very common phenomenon. Women are victimized not only outside their homes, but also within. Many of the crimes against women are perpetuated by people close to the women, in the very houses they live in. Female foeticide, female infanticide, child marriage, marital rape, wife battering, genital mutilation, harassment for dowry and dowry deaths, are all crimes directly linked to the home, as most of the crimes take place within the house. The home is no longer a safe haven for women. Domestic violence exists in various forms and includes physical, psychological, verbal, economic and sexual violence. What makes matters worse is the fact that the woman who is a victim of domestic violence often is offered little protection under the law. New laws need to be framed and old ones amended if women are to be protected. To make a point, the offence of marital rape has not been sufficiently accounted for in law. Rape is an offence which hinges on the absence of consent of the women. It should be realized that absence of consent does not have to be only in the form of a verbal 'No'. It should be assured and viewed from the context of the situation. Within a marriage or if a women gives consent to sexual intercourse because of various pressures, or threat of injury to self or the children, or fear of being kicked out of the house or economic deprivation it is still not valid consent. It is still rape. The law does not punish rape within marriage, if the woman is above fifteen years of age. Forced sexual intercourse is an offence only when the woman is living separately from her husband under judicial separation / custom. Till now, the law does not deal sufficiently with marital rape.

It can also be said that while the physical aspect of domestic violence is visible and physical injuries are easy to prove in court, mental and emotional violence, which is quite common in homes, is difficult to prove. India is one of the few countries that has a law to deal with mental violence which women have to face; which is covered under Section 498A of the Indian Penal Code, which reads as follows:

Husband or Relatives of Husband of a Woman subjecting her cruelty

Whoever, being the husband or relative of the husband of a woman, subjects such woman to cruelty shall be punished with imprisonment for a term which may extend to three years and shall also be liable for fine.

Explanation : For the purpose of this section, 'cruelty' means—

Any wilful conduct which is of such nature as is likely to drive the woman to commit suicide or to cause grave injury or danger to life, limb or health (whether physical or mental) of the woman; or

Harassment of the woman where such harassment is with the view to coercing her or any person related to her to meet any unlawful demand for any property or valuable security or is on account of failure by her or any person related to her to meet such a demand.

This provision recognizes the need to address and protect

a woman, not only in case of physical cruelty, but also mental cruelty. This aspect makes this a unique provision, not only in India, but in the world. But though the provision exists, and though a woman may be subjected to mental cruelty, there are no standardized tests or objective criteria, that can be used and applied to gauge the extent of mental cruelty faced by a woman. Courts in India have defined cruelty as necessarily involving a subjective element. Therefore, mental cruelty is largely determined by the individual judge before whom the case is filed. And it has been found that our male Judges often have a biased attitude against women, and the chauvinistic attitude of judges is very obvious. Though a number of instances and cases can be quoted, only one is being quoted. This attitude of judges is clear from the book of Justice J.D. Kapoor, (High Court of Delhi), *Laws and flaws in marriage—How to stay Happily Married* — some quotes from his book :

> "Women of Superior intelligence are generally torn between their feminity and their intellectuality. They are obsessed with the development of their career to such an extent that they are forever absorbed with themselves. It is mostly women who hold managerial or professional jobs who suffer from this syndrome, as they tend to lack the willingness to compromise. For them, even rearing children or raising a family is not a social obligation. A situation in which a woman considers herself intellectually superior is fraught with danger as there is always a likelihood of such a woman being fascinated by a person who is more capable than her husband".

If this is the frame of mind of an honourable judge of the High Court, one does not have to go to any length to know the fate of women (especially a professional woman) who stands in the court of law, asking and appealing for justice and redressing of her grievances.

In the same book (p. 70) his views on cruelty in marriage clearly show that he is of the opinion that men have the right to be cruel to women and that women should not make an issue of such cruelty and ask for divorce.

To quote from his book again about his views on cruelty—

> "For example, a wife was granted divorce because her husband, while sick, was indecent to her, choked her, struck her once and called her a whore. The divorce was allowed on the grounds of the husband single act of striking his wife in the face"

He believes that striking a woman, calling her a whore, being indecent to her, choking her "just once" are in a way not sufficient to grant her a divorce. Perhaps a woman should stay and bear all these things everyday, until one day she becomes mad or commits suicide, but not approach the court — this seems to be insinuation of the 'Honourable Judge'. If an educated person like a Judge, a person who is responsible for giving justice to a woman, holds this view; then what is the point of framing laws for the protection of woman and how far these laws will be effective in dealing with violence and crime against women is a question which needs serious deliberation.

Further, in a judgement delivered by justice J.D. Kapoor in 2003 in Savitri *Vs.* Ramesh Chandra and Others, it is clear that he feels that gender specific laws, such as section 498A of the Indian Penal Code are misused by Women and, therefore, such offences should be made bailable and non-cognizable. Though it may be granted that perhaps in numerous such cases, one odd case may be a case of misuse by a woman, it should be remembered that for lakhs of women, such laws offer a ray of hope and give them a feeling that in case of extreme harassment and torture, the country does have laws to protect them.

A number of laws have been framed for the protection, betterment and upliftment of women, but in spite of these laws, little has changed. In spite of the Hindu Marriage Act of 1955, in which monogamy was recognized as the legal form of marriage, polygamy is still prevalent in society; in spite of the Child Marriage Restraint Act, child marriage continues unabated, in spite of the Dowry Prohibition Act of 1961, dowry is increasing, so are the cases related to dowry harassment and dowry deaths. Many more laws and their ineffectiveness in improving the status of women can be quoted. Also, the loopholes in existing laws should be studied and plugged, so that they can be effective in providing protection to woman, for example if we take up the Dowry Prohibition Act we find that though this act was passed more than forty years back, it has not been able to check the menace of dowry, which instead of decreasing, is increasing every year.

This just goes to show that some steps need to be taken, to increase the efficacy of this law, like —

> One of the drawbacks of this act is that both the giver and taker of dowry are punishable under law. As a result, complaints for dowry harassment are not registered, as in such a case, the giver – i.e. the girls parents are also liable for punishment, for giving dowry. Hence, this is one aspect that needs looking into.

Usually at the time of marriage/immediately before or after marriage gifts and items given are displayed. This in a way increases the greed and expectations of people, who want that their sons should get more than what has been given and displayed. This display of gifts and items should be banned and *penalized*.

Though Section 8B of the Act specifically provides that the State governments may provide Dowry Prohibition Officers to ensure effective implementation of the Act, many States have not appointed such officers.

Even where these officers have been appointed in States, they are very few and not in a position to deal with a population of lakhs. Their number, therefore, should be increased. Also, people are not aware about the existence of such officers. This awareness needs to be created.

Section 8D(40) further states that the State governments may appoint an advisory board consisting of not more than five social workers (out of which at least two shall be women) to assist and advise the Dowry Prohibition Officers in exercising their jurisdiction under sub-section (1). But many States have failed to constitute such advisory boards. Just making laws is not enough. For effective implementation of the laws related to dowry, it is strongly recommended that such officers should be appointed in all the States and various districts of the State and boards set up, to provide relief to women and make the Dowry Prohibition Act more effective.

There are many laws related to women which should be deeply studied and amended, if required and loopholes plugged.

The Indian Law, in its present form is largely based on the British law and is the contribution of British rulers who did not fully understand the Indian Social System or Family System while framing the laws. The law has failed to appreciate the peculiar position of a wife in the family, as marriage and family did not have the same significance in British society as it has in the Indian Society. There was not adequate economic protection for the woman. For example, in case of Domestic Violence, the main problem is to restrain the husband from using violence. If the wife files a civil suit against her husband, the likelihood is that the suit may take years to settle. In the meantime, the wife often has no funds or separate place to stay in. Approaching the court against the husband may warrant more violence from the husband. Civil remedies do not provide immediate relief to the victim and they have hardly any preventive effect on the violent husbands. Therefore, enactment of provisions of law which may provide immediate protection without instituting a civil suit is required. In U.K. and the United States, non-molestation injunctions are issued in case of domestic violence, which restrain the husband from using violence against the wife. Such a provision should be made available to the victims of violence without requiring them to initiate a civil suit for some relief. In other words injunctions should not be attached with other remedies but should be used as an independent remedy. In case there is an imminent danger of physical abuse of the wife and in case of requirement of immediate protection, an expedited order in the form of a temporary civil protection, which is effective for a short time, should also be provided, to ensure the safety of the woman.

Under the law of England, a wife can also get the violent husband out of the house for a few days and get the law to restrain him from visiting the house or meeting the children. Breach of the order is punishable with arrest and fine. Similarly in England, if divorce is granted and the children are staying with the wife, then the matrimonial home is given to the wife to stay in and the husband has to shift elsewhere. This is a very strong deterrent to the husband, who has to think twice before using violence in the house, knowing fully well that his house will be taken from him. The woman too is not left shelterless and homeless, as also the children. Such a provision needs to be made in the Indian law too; if domestic violence has to be checked. Some of these provisions have been incorporated in the new law that has been framed (in 2005) to check domestic violence.

Many changes in the laws are required. In fact, crime against women should be treated as special crimes and offenders should be given harsher punishments, as has been observed by Justice Katju of the Allahabad High Court, while giving judgement in a case in which the head of the deceased women was literally battered by the murderer.

In case a man is found guilty of two offences against a woman on two occasions, then he must be awarded maximum punishment along with a heavy fine; which should be given to the woman.

Incest must be made an offence under the code. Incest is the worst possible immoral act, but it is not an offence under the code.

Cases related to women must be decided at the earliest and a maximum time limit of two years at the most should be provided to settle the case. No doubt Family Courts have been set up to deal with cases related to women, but even here the cases drag on for years and years. Evaluation of the cases of any Family Court will show that out of all the cases registered in the family court in a year, nearly half do not even get a first hearing.

If the domestic violence is to be checked and for the position of the women in our country to improve, it is obvious that there is a great and urgent need for changes in the law. These changes should not be confirmed or limited to any one Act or branch of the Indian Law. It should concern almost all branches of civil and criminal laws like the Penal Code, the Code of Criminal Procedure, the Civil Procedure Code, the Evidence Act, and special laws pertaining to women like the Child Marriage Act, Dowry Prohibition Act, Suppression of Immoral Traffic Act and others. New concepts regarding protection of women in the house, economic security, punishment to offenders and defaulters, imposition of fines and delays in courts, etc., have to be introduced and the concepts of jurisprudence and male superiority and leniency to accused have to be discarded.

One of the biggest loopholes in the legal system is in the system of jurisprudence, which lays the onus of providing the guilt of the accused on the prosecution. If the prosecution is unable to provide sufficient evidence (which is often difficult, as in crimes against women in the house, the only witnesses are often the husband and his relative who protect themselves in anyway, including tampering with the evidences and lying) the accused might just walk away. With the law and legal formalities heavily tilted in favour of the accused, prevention and punishment of crime and the accused becomes very difficult. In cases involving women, therefore, the onus of proving innocence should on the accused and the diction of 'guilty until provided innocent' should be followed. A similar presumption under section 306-IPC, in case of suicide should also be made, so that the tendency of being cruel to a woman and forcing her in a way to commit suicide is also checked.

Further, to help the police in performing their duties and bringing the culprit to book, confessions made before any police personnel should be admissible as evidence. It should not be mandatory to produce independent witnesses, which at present is one of the biggest flaws in the administration of criminal justice. Section 25 of the Indian Evidence Act must be scrapped in cases related to woman; recording of confessions by a police officer should render it admissible in evidence.

The law must remember that the woman victim has already suffered and been victimised. She must be protected from any further harassment or victimization, when she approaches the court of law for justice. Laws should be enacted not only to provide compensation to the victim but also protection to the victim and witnesses. She should be spared the tension and agony of prolonged investigations and a long drawn trial. Investigations and trials need to be expedited. To deter witnesses from retracting from their statements in court, sections 161 and 162 of Cr.P.C should be amended. The statements of witnesses signed by them should be made admissible in evidence. The different constituents of the machinery to enforce justice, like the forensic experts, the police personnel, judicial personnel must work together in harmony, to ensure that a woman who is victimised is granted relief and justice at the earliest and the people responsible for violence and crimes against women are brought to book and punished, so that violence and crimes against women can be prevented and checked. A new law to provide protection to women against Domestic Violence has been framed in 2005, but it is to be seen whether it goes the way of other such Acts related to women or whether it will succeed in preventing crime and violence against women in the house.

References

Agarwal, Sushila, *Status of Women* : Printwell Publishers, Jaipur, 1988.

Ahuja, Ram, *Crime Against Women*, Rawat Publications, Jaipur.

Altekar, A.S., *Position of Women In Hindu Civilization*, Motilal Banarasi Das, 1938.

Antoy, M.J. *Women's Rights;* Dialogue Publication, New Delhi, 1985.

Archer, J and Lloyd, *B., Sex and Gender;* Harmonds - Worth: Penguin, 1982.

Archor, M.S., *Women Society and Change* : McGraw Hill Book Company, New York, 1971.

Asthana, Pratima, *Women's Movement in India,* New Delhi: Vikas Publication, 1974.

Baig, Tara Ali, *India's Women Power* : S.Chand & Co. Pvt. Ltd., New Delhi, 1976.

Asia Human Resource in 21" Century and Beyond (Volume 4, Women and Globalisation): Sarup & Sons, New Delhi, 2001.

Bandwick, Judith, M. *Women in Transition;* The Harvest Press Ltd., Sussex, 1980.

Boserup, Ester, *Women's Role in Economic Development* : St. Martin's Press, New York, 1970.

Chanana, Karima, *Socialisation, Education and Women,* Orient Publication, New Delhi, 1985.

Chapman, Jane Roberts, *Economic Independence of Women,* Sage Publications, London, 1976.

Chattopadhayay, Kanladwi, *Indian Women's Battle for Freedom;* Abhinav Publications, New Delhi, 1983.

Cormack, Margaret, *The Hindu Women,* New York, 1953.

Crime in India, National Crime Records Bureau, Ministry of Home Affairs, Govt. of India, New Delhi, Annual Reports – 1998-2002.

Dak, T.M., *Women and Work in Indian Society,* Discovery Publishing House, Delhi, 1988.

Desai, Nena, *Women in Modern India,* Vohra & Co. Publishers Pvt. Ltd., Bombay, 1957.

Desai, Nena and Maithregi, Krishna Raj, *Women and Society in India,* Ajanta Publications, Delhi, 1987.

Devi, S, *Women's Status and Social Change,* Pointer Publishers, Jaipur, 1999.

Fleming, *Stopping Wife Abuse*, Doubleday Anchor Press, New York, 1979.

Gelles, Richard J., *Family Violence*, Sage Publications, New Bury, 1987.

Ghosh, S.K. *Women in a Changing Society,* Ashish Publishing House, New Delhi, 1984.

Gupta, Mukta. *'Issues Related to Women'*, Sarup & Sons, New Delhi.

Hate, Chandrakala; A. Changing Status of Women in Post Independence India; Allied Publishers, Bombay, 1969.

Kant, Anjali. *Women and Law* – A.P.H. Publishing Corporation, 2003, New Delhi.

Kapoor, J.D., '*Laws and Flaws in Marriage- How to Stay Happily : Married*, Konark Publishers, Delhi, 2002.

Kaushik, Sushila, *Women's Oppression- Patterns and Perspectives :* Shakti Books, Vikas, New Delhi, 1985.

Karlekar, Malavika, *Poverty and Women's Work,* Vikas Publishing House, New Delhi, 1982.

Majumdar, Maya. *Protecting Our Women*, Volumes I & II, Dominant Publishers and Distributors, New Delhi, 2002.

Maurya, S.D. *Women in India :* Chug Publications, Allahabad, 1988.

Mittal, Mukta, Woman Power in India; Anmol Pub., New Delhi, 1995.

Seth, Mira. *Women and Development : The Indian Experience,* Sage Publications, New Delhi, 2001.

Srinivas, M.N. *Changing Position of Indian Women,* Oxford University Press, New Delhi, 1978.

Srivastava, T.N., *Women and the Law,* Intellectual Publishing House, 1985.

Verma, H.N. and Amrit : *Women through the Ages:* Indian Publishers, New Delhi, 1976.

Yaqin, Anwarul and Anwar, *Badar, Protection of Women under Law;* An Annotated Bibliography, Deep & Deep Publications, New Delhi, 1982.

Index